SEARCH ENGINE OPTIMIZATION (SEO)

DE COMPREHENSIVE, MODERN GUIDE THAT INCLUDES ALL ADVANCED TACTICS & PRACTICAL STRATEGIES TO HELP YOU LEARN MORE QUICKLY & BOOST YOUR VISIBILITY & ORGANIC SEARCH RANKS.

RICHARD N. WILLIAMS

TABLE OF CONTENTS

Definition of SEO..3
Importance of Organic Search Rankings................................3
Chapter 1...3
Key SEO Concepts..3
Keywords and their relevance..3
On-Page Optimization and Off-Page Optimization................3
Backlinks and Link Building..3
Chapter 2...3
Technical SEO..3
Website Structure and Navigation...3
URL Structure and Mobile Optimization................................3
Page Speed and Performance..3
Chapter 3...3
Content Optimization...3
Quality Content Creation...3
Content Relevance and Engagement..3
Multimedia Integration..3
Chapter 4...3
User Experience (UX) and SEO..3
Importance of UX in Search Rankings....................................3
Navigation and Accessibility...3
Responsive Design..3
Chapter 5...3
Local SEO...3
Importance of Local Search...3
Google My Business Optimization..3
Local Citations and Reviews...3
Chapter 6...3
SEO Analytics and Measurement..3
Key Metrics to Track and Tools for SEO Analysis................3
Monitoring and Adjusting Strategies.......................................3
Chapter 7...3
Emerging Trends in SEO..3

Voice Search Optimization..3
Featured Snippets and Position Zero 3
AI and Machine Learning in SEO 3
Chapter 8...3
Case Studies Successful SEO Campaigns 3
Lessons Learned from SEO Failures 3
CONCLUSION 3
Strategies and Continuous Adaptation in SEO.................3
INTRODUCTION 1

INTRODUCT ION

In the clamoring city of Digitalville, Imprint, a decided business visionary, ended up exploring the serious scene of the web-based market. Outfitted with a visionary soul and a resolute obligation to his startup, Imprint dove into the universe of Website optimization - an excursion that would change his business in manners he would never have envisioned.

Imprint's organization, TechInnovate Arrangements, started like numerous new companies, confronting the test of hanging out in the huge ocean of advanced stages. Mark realized that just having an online presence would not be enough to succeed; perceivability and importance were the keys to progress in the computerized domain.

He set out on a journey to disentangle the secrets of Search engine optimization, remembering it as the key part for natural development. As opposed to surrendering to the intricacies of the algorithmic labyrinth, Imprint moved toward Search engine optimization as a craftsmanship, mixing imagination with vital understanding.

The realization that the most important thing was to know who the target audience was led TechInnovate to its first breakthrough. Imprint and his group fastidiously broke down client conduct, inclinations, and search designs. This information driven approach made ready for customized content that reverberated with the crowd, making way for a drawing in client experience.

Embracing the force of watchwords, Imprint streamlined the site's substance, consistently incorporating significant terms that reflected the language of TechInnovate's possible clients. Because of its increased relevance in search engine results, the website transformed into a virtual beacon and began to attract organic traffic.

As the computerized scene advanced, Imprint stayed watchful, adjusting his Search engine optimization systems to the evolving calculations. The versatile soul of TechInnovate was reflected in its deftness to remain on the ball. Mark embraced development, exploring different avenues regarding new procedures and instruments to refine the organization's Website design enhancement approach.

One significant second came when Imprint found the capability of backlinks. Understanding the significance of laying out validity in the computerized biological system, he fashioned vital associations with powerhouses and industry pioneers. The far reaching influence of these partnerships flowed through the web, catapulting TechInnovate's perceivability and authority.

In the constantly advancing universe of Search engine optimization, remaining informed was Imprint's distinct advantage. He ate up industry bits of

3

knowledge, went to gatherings, and drew in with Website optimization networks. This obligation to constant learning not just kept TechInnovate at the front line of patterns yet additionally situated Imprint as an idea chief in the Search engine optimization domain.

TechInnovate's example of overcoming adversity wasn't just about climbing web crawler rankings; It was evidence of the transformative effects of SEO on a company as well as Mark's unwavering dedication. TechInnovate's products seamlessly met the needs of its expanding audience on TechInnovate's website, which evolved into a digital innovation hub.

The success of TechInnovate's SEO was felt not only online but also in the tangible expansion of the company. The organization's income took off, and its market presence extended dramatically. Clients and accomplices ran to the brand, attracted by the realness and worth passed on through its internet based presence.

Imprint's excursion with Website optimization wasn't without challenges. There were calculation refreshes that shook the groundworks of advanced procedures, and contenders competed for the best position. However, TechInnovate's greatest strengths were its resilience and adaptability. Mark saw difficulties as opportunities to innovate and improve his SEO strategy rather than obstacles.

Eventually, the extraordinary force of Website optimization went past further developing inquiry rankings; it reshaped the account of TechInnovate. The once-obscure startup became a digital beacon of innovation and dependability, leaving an imprint on its sector.

Imprint moving excursion instructs us that in the powerful universe of online business, embracing Web optimization is in excess of a procedure; it's a mentality. It's tied in with figuring out your crowd, adjusting to change, and continually developing. Through his immovable obligation to Search engine optimization greatness, Imprint moved TechInnovate higher than ever as well as roused an age of computerized business visionaries to leave on their own extraordinary excursions.

Definition of SEO

Site improvement (Web optimization) is a complex discipline that assumes a vital part in the computerized scene, forming the internet based perceivability and progress of sites. At its center, Web optimization is the act of enhancing web content to further develop its positioning on web crawler results pages (SERPs). This complex cycle includes a blend of specialized, imaginative, and scientific systems pointed toward upgrading a site's importance and authority according to web indexes.

In a general sense, Website optimization spins around three key support points:

Specialized Search engine optimization: This perspective spotlights on streamlining the specialized components of a site to work on its crawlability, indexation, and in general execution. Components, for example, site speed, versatile responsiveness, and a protected HTTPS association are necessary parts of specialized Website optimization. Guaranteeing that web search tool bots can effectively slither and file a site's substance is central, as it establishes the groundwork for higher perceivability.

On-Page Web optimization: This feature manages enhancing individual pages to make them more interesting to the two clients and web crawlers. Watchword research, content enhancement, and the utilization of meta labels are fundamental components of on-page Web optimization. Creating superior grade, significant substance with decisively positioned watchwords assists web crawlers with figuring out the setting of a page, at last adding to further developed rankings.

Off-Page Search engine optimization: While on-page Web optimization centers around upgrading the substance and construction of a site, off-page Website optimization is worried about outer variables that impact a webpage's validity and authority. Backlinks, social signs, and online standing administration fall under this class. A website's authority in the eyes of search engines is largely determined by the quantity and quality of its inbound links from other trustworthy websites.

Key Parts of Web optimization:
Catchphrase
Exploration: Distinguishing and focusing on the right catchphrases is the groundwork of Website optimization. SEO professionals conduct extensive research to identify the terms and phrases that users are most likely to

enter into search engines. These catchphrases then, at that point, guide content creation and improvement endeavors.

Creation of Content: Superior grade, applicable substance is essential to Website optimization achievement. The goal of search engines is to deliver content that is useful and instructive to users. By making content that tends to client expectation and gives answers for their questions, sites can situate themselves as definitive sources in their separate specialties.

Building links: The amount and nature of inbound connections essentially influence a site's position and web crawler rankings. Building a strong backlink profile includes procuring joins from trustworthy sites inside a similar industry. Outreach, building relationships, and the creation of shareable content are all necessary parts of this procedure.

Client Experience (UX): A positive client experience is an essential component in Website optimization. Web indexes focus on sites that offer a consistent and easy to understand insight. Factors, for example, page load speed, portable responsiveness, and natural route add to a positive client experience.

Monitoring and Analytics: Web optimization is a continuous cycle that requires consistent checking and change. Using examination devices gives bits of knowledge into site execution, client conduct, and the adequacy of Website optimization procedures. Standard investigation empowers Web optimization experts to adjust their methodology in light of information driven bits of knowledge.

Advancement of Website design enhancement:

SEO has changed a lot over time to keep up with changes in user behavior and algorithms used by search engines. Early Web optimization techniques frequently spun around catchphrase stuffing and manipulative strategies to fool web indexes into positioning a site higher. In any case, as web crawlers turned out to be more complex, accentuation moved towards conveying quality substance and a positive client experience.

The approach of AI and computerized reasoning has additionally changed Search engine optimization. Web search tools like Google utilize complex calculations that consider many elements to decide rankings. Figuring out client aim and giving pertinent, definitive substance has become central in the cutting edge Website optimization scene.

Challenges in Website optimization:

Website optimization isn't without its difficulties. Search engine algorithms are constantly evolving, necessitating constant adaptation. Staying aware of industry patterns, calculation refreshes, and arising advancements is vital for Website optimization experts. Moreover, the serious idea of online spaces implies that remaining ahead frequently includes a dynamic and vital methodology.

SEO's Effect on Businesses:

For organizations, a strong Web optimization system can be a distinct advantage. Higher web crawler rankings mean expanded perceivability, natural traffic, and possible clients. Further developed web-based presence improves brand believability and trust among clients. Furthermore, compelling Web optimization can prompt a more productive and easy to understand site, adding to in general business achievement.

The online success of websites is significantly influenced by SEO, a dynamic and multifaceted field. From specialized improvement to content creation and third party referencing, the different parts of Web optimization cooperate to upgrade a site's perceivability and authority on web crawlers. As innovation keeps on developing, Website optimization will without a doubt stay a foundation of computerized showcasing methodologies, molding the manner in which organizations associate with their interest groups in the immense scene of the web.

Importance of Organic Search Rankings

Natural hunt rankings assume an urgent part in the web-based perceivability and progress of organizations today. As the computerized scene keeps on developing, web search tools like Google stay the essential passage for clients looking for data, items, and administrations. Understanding the significance of natural inquiry rankings is urgent for organizations expecting to lay out major areas of strength for a presence and interface with their interest group really.

Natural hunt rankings, first and foremost, straightforwardly influence site traffic. A website is more likely to get more clicks if it appears on the first page of search engine results. Research reliably shows that clients will quite often tap on the initial not many outcomes, making it basic for organizations to enhance their substance and site for natural pursuit. This expanded perceivability drives more traffic as well as improves the believability of a site according to clients.

Besides, natural inquiry is a savvy system contrasted with paid promotion. While paid promotions can give quick perceivability, they include some major disadvantages. Interestingly, natural hunt depends on advancing substance, further developing site structure, and carrying out Website optimization best practices. In spite of the fact that it demands investment and exertion, the drawn out advantages of natural pursuit, like supported perceivability and believability, offset the underlying speculation.

Rankings in organic searches are more important than just getting people to your website. It has a direct impact on brand trust and credibility. Clients intrinsically trust sites that show up at the highest point of natural list items, thinking of them as more solid and legitimate. It is essential to produce high-quality, relevant content on a consistent basis that is in line with user intent in order to build and maintain this trust, which will ultimately result in increased customer loyalty and retention.

Besides, natural hunting is instrumental in contacting a designated crowd. By upgrading content for explicit watchwords and expressions, organizations can fit their internet based presence to match the interests and needs of their optimal clients. This designated approach guarantees that the right crowd finds the business, improving the probability of changing over guests into clients. Businesses can create content that resonates with their audience and fosters engagement and relationships by understanding the search intent behind keywords.

Natural inquiry rankings likewise add to a positive client experience. Web crawlers focus on sites that offer significant, easy to understand content. A website's organic search performance is influenced by factors such as page load speed, mobile responsiveness, and relevance of the content. Putting resources into these perspectives further develops rankings as well as upgrades the general client experience, bringing about fulfilled guests who are bound to remain on the site and investigate its contributions.

As well as drawing in likely clients, natural pursuit rankings can likewise impact buying choices. At the point when clients look for items or administrations, they frequently lead examinations to analyze choices. Organizations that reliably show up in natural list items construct serious areas of strength for a presence, impacting purchasers at different phases of the purchasing venture. Being noticeable during the examination stage improves the probability of being considered during the dynamic interaction, at last prompting transformations.

Besides, natural pursuit rankings are an impression of a site's pertinence and authority inside its industry. To determine a website's authority, search engines look at a variety of factors, such as the quality of the content, social signals, and backlinks. Businesses can become industry leaders by consistently producing valuable content and establishing a robust online presence. Not only does this increase organic traffic, but it also opens doors to industry collaborations, partnerships, and other opportunities.

All in all, the significance of natural hunt rankings couldn't possibly be more significant in the computerized age. Organic search plays a crucial role in the online success of businesses in a variety of ways, including increasing website traffic, establishing brand credibility, and influencing purchasing decisions. By putting resources into Website optimization procedures, organizations can improve their web-based presence, associate with their interest group, and remain cutthroat in an undeniably advanced commercial center.

Chapter 1
Key SEO
Concepts

Website streamlining (Web optimization) is a dynamic and fundamental part of computerized promoting that spins around upgrading a site to work on its perceivability on web search tool results pages (SERPs). Understanding key Search engine optimization ideas is critical for organizations and site proprietors trying to improve their internet based presence and draw in natural rush hour gridlock. This article will dig into essential Web optimization rules that add to a site's web crawler positioning.

1. Keywords: The Building Blocks of SEO Keywords are the foundation of SEO. When looking for information, these are the terms or phrases that users type into search engines. Directing careful catchphrase research recognizes significant and high-traffic watchwords for your substance. Key situation of these catchphrases in titles, headings, and all through the substance signs to web crawlers that your page is a significant asset for clients.

2. On-Page Streamlining: Creating Easy to understand Content On-page enhancement includes advancing individual pages to further develop their web crawler rankings. This incorporates streamlining title labels, meta portrayals, headings, and content. Utilizing appropriate HTML tags and structuring content in a logical hierarchy not only improves readability for users but also assists search engines in comprehending your content's context and relevance.

3. Quality Substance: The Head honcho of Website optimization Making superior grade, significant substance is at the center of Web optimization achievement. Web indexes focus on satisfaction that tends to clients' questions, gives important experiences, and is elegantly composed. Routinely refreshing and extending your substance signs to web crawlers that your webpage is dynamic and important, adding to further developed rankings after some time.

4. Backlinks: Building Authority and Trust

Backlinks are joins from different sites to yours. Web search tools consider these as demonstrations of approval in your substance. Nonetheless, not all backlinks are made equivalent. Quality and pertinence are vital. Linking to your content from authoritative websites can significantly improve your search engine rankings. Building a different and normal backlink profile requires a mix of content quality, effort, and relationship working inside your industry.

5. Specialized Web optimization: Guaranteeing Web search tool Crawlers Can Explore Your Webpage Specialized Web optimization centers around streamlining the specialized parts of your site to upgrade its crawlability and indexability via web search tools. This incorporates enhancing site speed, carrying out a sitemap, using robots.txt documents, and guaranteeing legitimate URL structures. A very much upgraded specialized establishment helps web index crawlers as well as improves the general client experience.

6. Versatile Plan: An Unquestionable necessity for Website design enhancement Achievement

With the rising utilization of cell phones, having a versatile site is basic for Website design enhancement. Web crawlers focus on portable responsive locales, and having a responsive plan guarantees that your site looks and works well on different gadgets. Google, specifically, utilizes versatile first ordering, meaning it essentially involves the portable adaptation of the substance for ordering and positioning.

7. Experience for Users: The Quiet Web optimization Patron Client experience (UX) assumes a critical part in Website design enhancement. Web indexes mean to furnish clients with the most ideal outcomes, and a positive client experience adds to higher rankings. Factors, for example, page load speed, route simplicity, and portable responsiveness all affect the general client experience. Guaranteeing a consistent and charming experience for guests can in a roundabout way support your Website design enhancement endeavors.

8. Neighborhood Website design enhancement: Focusing on Nearby Crowds For organizations with an actual presence, nearby Website design enhancement is critical. This includes enhancing your internet based presence for neighborhood look, including making a Google My Business profile, getting on the web surveys, and guaranteeing exact business data across online indexes. Neighborhood Web optimization assists organizations with showing up in nearby query items and on map postings, expanding perceivability for clients nearby.

9. Calculation Updates: Adapting to Changes in Search Engines Search engines are always improving their algorithms to deliver more relevant and accurate results. It is essential for maintaining and improving search rankings to remain informed about algorithm updates, particularly those issued by major search engines like Google. Adjusting your Search engine optimization technique because of these updates guarantees that your site remains upgraded for flow positioning rules.

10. Examination and Observing: Estimating Web optimization Achievement Executing instruments like Google Examination permits you to screen the presentation of your site and the viability of your Website optimization endeavors. Key metrics like organic traffic, bounce rates, and conversion rates can be tracked to learn what's working well and what needs to be improved. Ordinary examination and change of your Search engine optimization technique in light of information driven bits of knowledge add to supported achievement.

All in all, dominating key Web optimization ideas is fundamental for anybody hoping to lay out serious areas of strength for a presence. From watchword research and on-page improvement to building backlinks and adjusting to calculation refreshes, an exhaustive comprehension of these ideas engages site proprietors to explore the mind boggling scene of web index rankings. In the highly competitive world of online visibility, businesses and individuals can achieve sustainable success by consistently implementing and adapting these principles.

Keywords and their relevance

Keywords are a crucial part of modern communication, from academic research to internet search engines. These terms or expressions act as the key part interfacing clients to pertinent data in the huge region of computerized content. Understanding the meaning of watchwords is urgent for powerful correspondence, online perceivability, and data recovery.

In the domain of web search tools, watchwords go about as the passage among clients and the tremendous ocean of online substance. At the point when people type a question into a web index, the calculation examines the web for pages containing the predetermined watchwords. The importance and recurrence of these watchwords decide the positioning and perceivability of a page in list items. This highlights the significance of picking the right catchphrases to improve content for web indexes — a training known as site improvement (Web optimization).

In the computerized advertising scene, catchphrases are the groundwork of effective missions. Advertisers carefully research and select watchwords that line up with their interest group's pursuit conduct. By decisively integrating these catchphrases into site content, blog entries, and commercials, organizations can upgrade their web-based perceivability and draw in possible clients. Successful watchword research further develops web crawler rankings as well as guarantees that showcasing endeavors are customized to address the particular necessities and interests of the main interest group.

In scholar and logical settings, watchwords are key to sorting out and arranging research. To make it easier for other researchers to find and cite their findings, authors carefully select keywords that summarize the core of their work. This training smoothes out the tremendous assortment of academic writing, permitting researchers to proficiently explore through the ocean of data more. Besides, information bases and scholarly diaries use catchphrases to record and order articles, working with exact pursuits and advancing interdisciplinary exploration.

With regards to content creation, catchphrases assume an essential part in making drawing in and discoverable material. Journalists and content makers decisively incorporate applicable watchwords to make their substance more available to their interest group. Whether it's a blog entry, virtual entertainment update, or video script, the cautious determination and position of watchwords add to the discoverability of content, empowering it to contact a more extensive crowd.

Watchwords likewise play a critical part in the quickly developing scene of voice search. Understanding the subtleties of spoken language and common questions becomes increasingly important as more people use devices like smart speakers and virtual assistants. Improving substance for voice search includes considering the regular language that clients utilize, going for the golden conversational tone, and integrating long-tail watchwords that reflect normal spoken phrases. In spite of the shifting dynamics of search behavior, this adaptation makes certain that content remains relevant and accessible.

The importance of watchwords stretches out past the advanced domain into different expert fields. In the domain of data recovery, bookkeepers and filers depend on catchphrases to arrange and coordinate tremendous measures of information. Listing frameworks, both physical and computerized, use watchwords to make a productive and easy to understand framework for finding assets. This training works with the conservation and availability of data in libraries, chronicles, and computerized vaults.

All in all, watchwords are the key part of present day correspondence, assuming a focal part in data recovery, online perceivability, and powerful happy creation. Whether directing clients through the far reaching computerized scene or working with scholastic examination, the essential utilization of catchphrases is a foundation of effective correspondence in the 21st hundred years. As innovation proceeds to progress and correspondence channels advance, understanding and adjusting to the elements of watchwords stay fundamental for people and associations trying to explore and flourish in the always extending domain of data.

On-Page Optimization and Off-Page Optimization

On-Page Streamlining and Off-Page Improvement are two key mainstays of site improvement (Web optimization), working couple to upgrade a site's perceivability, importance, and in general execution in web crawler results. Let's get into the specifics of each to learn about their unique roles and significance in the digital landscape.

On-Page Enhancement:

On-Page Improvement alludes to the systems and strategies utilized straightforwardly on a site to upgrade its perceivability and pertinence to web crawlers. It includes upgrading different components inside the actual site to further develop its web index positioning. Here are key parts of On-Page Streamlining:

Watchword Exploration and Arrangement:

Directing careful watchword research is the groundwork of On-Page Enhancement. It includes recognizing pertinent watchwords that clients are probably going to look for. When distinguished, these catchphrases are decisively positioned in key region of the site, for example, the title tag, meta portrayal, headers, and all through the substance. This makes it easier for search engines to determine the content's relevance to queries made by users.

Content Quality and Significance:

Superior grade, applicable substance is urgent for On-Page Enhancement. Content that is beneficial to users is given priority by search engines. This includes text that is written well, has information, is interesting, and meets the needs of the users. Content ought to consolidate the distinguished catchphrases normally, keeping away from watchword stuffing.

Titles, Meta Descriptions, and Tags:

Title labels and meta portrayals assume a crucial part in drawing in clients and speaking with web search tools. Advancing these components includes creating convincing, succinct titles and portrayals that precisely address the substance of the page. Remembering watchwords for these labels can help the page's perceivability.

URL Construction:

A spotless and coordinated URL structure adds to a positive client experience and helps web crawlers in grasping the pecking order of a site. Remembering important watchwords for URLs can likewise add to On-Page Streamlining.

Header Labels (H1, H2, and so forth.):

Appropriate utilization of header labels works on the lucidness of the substance as well as signs the significance of various areas to web search tools. The page's main topic or keyword should be in the H1 tag, while subheadings (H2, H3, etc.) can give extra design.

Pictures and Sight and sound Improvement:

Enhancing pictures includes utilizing expressive document names, adding alt text, and packing pictures to further develop page stacking speed. Media components, when utilized in a calculated manner, can improve client commitment and contribute decidedly to On-Page Web optimization.

Dynamic Plan:

On-Page Optimization requires a responsive and mobile-friendly design because more and more people access websites via mobile devices. Google thinks about versatility as a positioning component.

Off-Page Improvement:

While On-Page Improvement centers around components inside the site, Off-Page Streamlining includes exercises outside the site to upgrade its position, validity, and notoriety. Here are key parts of Off-Page Improvement:

Building links:

Maybe the most notable part of Off-Page Improvement, external link establishment includes procuring top notch inbound connections from other trustworthy sites. These connections go about as "demonstrations of positive support" for a site's substance, indicating to web crawlers that the substance is significant and dependable.

Using Social Media:

Off-Page Optimization is significantly influenced by social media. Laying out areas of strength for an on stages like Facebook, Twitter, and LinkedIn increments brand perceivability as well as gives chances to content sharing. Social signs, like likes, offers, and remarks, are considered via web search tools.

Social Bookmarking:
Submitting content to social bookmarking destinations can upgrade perceivability and drive traffic. Sites like Reddit, Digg, and StumbleUpon permit clients to bookmark and offer substance, adding to Off-Page Website design enhancement endeavors.

Powerhouse Effort:
Working with industry influencers can help you get more exposure and valuable backlinks. Forces to be reckoned with frequently have a critical following, and their support can emphatically influence a site's validity.

Mentions of Brands:
Indeed, even without an immediate connection, the brand makes reference to different sites added to Off-Page Enhancement. Web search tools perceive brand specifications as signs of a site's power and significance inside its specialty.

Guest blogging:
In addition to establishing your expertise, contributing high-quality content to other websites in your field offers opportunities for backlinks. Visitor posting ought to zero in on legitimate sites with a pertinent crowd.

Review sites:
Positive web-based surveys on stages like Google My Business, Cry, and industry-explicit audit destinations add to a site's believability. When

determining a company's trustworthiness, search engines take into account online reviews.

All in all, On-Page Enhancement and Off-Page Streamlining are fundamental parts of a far reaching Website optimization methodology. While On-Page endeavors guarantee that a site's substance is important, very much organized, and easy to understand, Off-Page exercises center around building the site's position and believability through outer signs like backlinks, social commitment, and online notices. A comprehensive methodology that consolidates the two perspectives is fundamental for making supported progress in the cutthroat web-based scene.

Backlinks and Link Building

The Mainstays of Web optimization Achievement

In the steadily developing scene of web based showcasing and site improvement (Web optimization), backlinks and third party referencing stand as essential parts that can fundamentally influence a site's perceivability and positioning on web search tool results pages (SERPs). Understanding the subtleties of these ideas is critical for anybody hoping to improve their advanced presence and drive natural traffic to their internet based resources.

The Nuts and bolts of Backlinks

Backlinks, otherwise called inbound or approaching connections, are hyperlinks that point starting with one site then onto the next. These links, which indicate to search engines that the linked content is valuable and pertinent, function similarly to site-to-site votes of confidence. Google and other web indexes utilize these signs to evaluate the power, believability, and prevalence of a page.

Sorts of Backlinks

Regular Connections: Acquired naturally, these connections result from different sites viewing as your substance significant and connecting to it willfully.

Manual or Effort Connections: Gained through deliberate endeavors, these connections include effort to different sites, mentioning them to connect to your substance.

Self-Made Connections: Created by the site proprietor, these connections incorporate index entries, discussion marks, and remarks on websites.

Publication Connections: Given by site editors or content designers in view of the value of the substance.

The Significance of Backlinks

Web search tool Positioning: Web indexes consider backlinks as a demonstration of positive support. Websites with a greater number of high-quality backlinks frequently achieve higher rankings in SERPs.

Authority Building: Backlinks add to the power and validity of a site. It increases the trustworthiness of your website if other trustworthy websites link to it.

Reference Traffic: Backlinks further develop web search tool perceivability as well as get immediate traffic from clients tapping on the connection.

The Third party referencing Interaction

Third party referencing is the proactive methodology of procuring backlinks to work on a site's perceivability and authority. A powerful external link establishment crusade includes a few key stages.

1. Content Creation:

Delivering superior grade, useful, and shareable substance establishes the groundwork for fruitful external link establishment. Content that tackles issues, responds to questions, or engages is bound to draw in backlinks.

2. Recognizing Connection Open doors:

It's important to do research to find niche-specific websites and platforms that could link to your content. Devices like Ahrefs, Moz, and SEMrush can help in this cycle.

3. Effort and Relationship Building:

Drawing in with other site proprietors, bloggers, and powerhouses in your industry is fundamental. Building connections can prompt regular backlinks and cooperation potential open doors.

4. Visitor Posting:

Contributing important substance to different sites in return for a backlink is a typical third party referencing strategy. Visitor posting helps in contacting new crowds and laying out experts in your field.

5. Web-based Entertainment Advancement:

Utilizing virtual entertainment stages to share your substance builds its perceivability and the probability of others connecting to it.

Best Practices for Viable External link establishment

Center around Higher expectations without ever compromising: A couple of excellent backlinks from legitimate destinations can be more significant than various bad quality connections.

Relevance is Critical: Guarantee that the sites connecting to yours are applicable to your industry or specialty. Backlinks that don't matter could be interpreted as spam.

Various Anchor Text: Utilize an assortment of anchor texts while building backlinks. This gives a more normal profile and tries not to set off web crawler punishments.

Screen and Repudiate: Always keep an eye on your backlink profile and remove any links that are harmful or spammy. Maintaining a clean and reputable link profile is made easier by this.

Remain Informed About Calculation Updates: The algorithms of search engines are frequently updated. Remaining informed about these progressions helps in adjusting your external link establishment systems likewise.

Challenges and Moral Contemplations

While backlinks and third party referencing are significant for Web optimization achievement, there are moves and moral contemplations to be aware of. The overemphasis on connect amount over quality, dark cap Website design enhancement procedures like purchasing joins, and the gamble of punishments for manipulative practices are worries that Search engine optimization experts should explore.

a website's online presence is heavily influenced by backlinks and link building. A vital and moral way to deal with getting backlinks can fundamentally help a site's position, web search tool rankings, and by and large outcome in the computerized scene. As web crawlers keep on refining their calculations, remaining informed about prescribed procedures and adjusting to the developing Web optimization scene becomes basic for anybody looking for manageable internet based perceivability.

Chapter 2
Technical
SEO

Technical SEO is a critical aspect of search engine optimization that focuses on optimizing a website's infrastructure to improve its visibility and performance in search engine rankings. While content and backlinks play crucial roles in SEO, technical SEO ensures that search engines can crawl, index, and understand a website efficiently. In this comprehensive guide, we'll explore the key components of technical SEO and why they are essential for a website's success.

**1. Crawlability and Indexation:

One of the foundational elements of technical SEO is ensuring that search engines can crawl and index your website effectively. This involves creating a clear and organized site structure, utilizing XML sitemaps, and implementing robots.txt files. A well-structured site ensures that search engine bots can navigate through your content easily, indexing relevant pages and ignoring unnecessary ones.

2. Website Speed and Performance:
Page speed is a basic consideration for both client experience and web index rankings.Slow-loading pages can result in higher bounce rates and decreased user satisfaction. Technical SEO involves optimizing images, leveraging browser caching, and utilizing content delivery networks (CDNs) to enhance website speed. Google's PageSpeed Insights tool is a valuable resource for evaluating and improving page performance.

3. Mobile Optimization:
With the increasing use of mobile devices, Google has shifted to mobile-first indexing, prioritizing mobile-friendly websites in search results. Technical SEO includes ensuring responsive web design, optimizing images for mobile, and implementing Accelerated Mobile Pages (AMP) to create a seamless experience for mobile users.

4. Website Structure and URL Optimization:
A clear and logical website structure not only aids users in navigating your site but also helps search engines understand the hierarchy of your content. Technical SEO involves optimizing URLs, using descriptive

slugs, and creating a hierarchy of categories and subcategories. This not only enhances user experience but also facilitates search engine crawlers in understanding the context of each page.

5. Canonicalization:

Duplicate content can harm your SEO efforts by confusing search engines about which version of a page to index. Canonicalization involves specifying the preferred version of a page to search engines, reducing the risk of duplicate content issues. Implementing canonical tags correctly can prevent indexing problems and consolidate the SEO value of similar pages.

6. Schema Markup:

Schema markup is a code that provides search engines with additional information about the content on a page. By using schema markup, you can enhance the way your content appears in search results, providing rich snippets that include details like ratings, reviews, and event information. This not only improves the visibility of your content but also makes it more attractive to users.

7. SSL and HTTPS:

Security is a top priority for search engines, and having a secure website is now a ranking factor. Implementing Secure Sockets Layer (SSL) and using Hypertext Transfer Protocol Secure (HTTPS) encrypts data transmitted between the user's browser and the website, ensuring a secure connection. This not only boosts your search engine rankings but also builds trust with users.

8. Structured Data:

Structured data markup, often referred to as schema.org markup, helps search engines understand the context of your content. By providing additional information about your content, such as product details, event dates, or business information, you make it easier for search engines to deliver relevant results to users.

9. Redirects and Broken Links:

Managing redirects and fixing broken links are crucial for a smooth user experience and maintaining SEO health. Technical SEO involves setting up proper redirects when you change URLs and regularly checking for broken links. This ensures that users and search engine crawlers can navigate through your site without encountering dead ends.

10. Website Accessibility:

An accessible website is not only essential for users with disabilities but also contributes to better SEO. Technical SEO includes optimizing your website for accessibility, ensuring that all users, regardless of their abilities, can access and understand your content. This involves using descriptive alt text for images, creating readable text, and providing transcripts for multimedia content.

technical SEO is a multifaceted discipline that plays a crucial role in determining a website's success in search engine rankings. By addressing the technical aspects outlined in this guide, you can create a solid foundation for your website's SEO strategy.

From ensuring crawlability and indexation to optimizing page speed, mobile experience, and security, each element contributes to a website's overall performance in search engine results. As search algorithms continue to evolve, staying on top of technical SEO best practices is essential for maintaining and improving your website's visibility and relevance.

Website Structure and Navigation

Site design and route assume an essential part in making an easy to use online experience. An efficient and natural design not just improves the stylish allure of a site yet in addition straightforwardly influences client commitment and fulfillment. In this investigation, we will dig into the critical parts of successful site construction and route, underscoring their significance in forming a positive client venture.

1. Clear Order and Data Design:
A strong starting point for any site starts with a reasonable pecking order and data engineering. This entails logically categorizing content and establishing a hierarchy that seamlessly directs users through the website. A clear cut structure assists guests with understanding where to find explicit data and how various segments connect with one another. This clearness helps with diminishing skip rates and improves the probability of clients remaining on the site for longer terms.

2. Instinctive Route Menus:

Route menus act as the guide for clients investigating a site. They ought to be instinctive, effectively open, and unmistakably shown. Essential route menus, typically situated at the highest point of a page, ought to incorporate key segments or pages. Sub-menus can add more levels of hierarchy, allowing users to easily navigate through complex content. Distinct names and clear classification add to a positive client experience, forestalling disarray and disappointment.

3. Responsive Plan for Different Gadgets:

In the time of different gadget use, a responsive plan is basic. Sites should adjust consistently to different screen sizes, including work areas, PCs, tablets, and cell phones. Responsive plan takes care of a more extensive crowd as well as improves client fulfillment by giving a steady encounter across gadgets. Components like folding menus and adaptable designs add to the flexibility of the site, guaranteeing openness for clients no matter what their favored gadget.

4. Client Driven Search Usefulness:

While viable route menus are significant, a hearty inquiry usefulness further enables clients to rapidly see as unambiguous substance. The search process is streamlined when a user-centric search bar with predictive suggestions and filters is implemented. Consolidating savvy calculations upgrades the precision of query items, further developing client fulfillment by limiting the time and exertion expected to find data.

5. Reliable Marking Components:

Consistency in marking components, for example, logos, variety plans, and typography, adds to a firm and expert appearance. Clients ought to effectively perceive a site's image character across various pages. This consistency encourages trust as well as helps in route, as clients partner explicit plan components with specific segments or activities, making a visual aide all through their excursion.

6. Attractive Homepage:

The landing page fills in as a virtual retail facade, offering clients an underlying look into the site's substance and reason. It ought to be connecting with, giving a preview of key data and directing clients toward their areas of interest.

Intelligent components, convincing visuals, and succinct suggestions to take action can empower further investigation. A very much planned landing page establishes the vibe for the client experience and urges guests to dive further into the site.

7. Effective Cross-Linking and Linking:

A website's connectivity is enhanced by cross-linking between related pages and strategic linking within the content. Interior connections guide clients to significant data, advancing a more vivid encounter. Furthermore, web search tools esteem very much organized connecting, adding to further developed Web optimization rankings.

Be that as it may, finding some kind of harmony is urgent; exorbitant connecting can be overpowering and counterproductive, possibly prompting client disarray.

8. Considering Accessibility:

A website that is accessible to users of all abilities is inclusive. Openness contemplations, like alt text for pictures, console route choices, and clear headings, guarantee that people with handicaps can explore and consume content flawlessly. Focusing on openness lines up with moral guidelines as well as grows the likely crowd for a site.

9. Execution Streamlining:

Effective site execution is vital to a positive client experience. Fast stacking times, negligible server mistakes, and smooth associations add to client fulfillment. Upgrading pictures, using content conveyance organizations (CDNs), and carrying out reserving instruments are techniques that improve execution, forestalling client dissatisfaction because of slow or lethargic sites.

10. Client Input and Iterative Improvement:

Executing instruments for client input, like studies and investigation, permits site proprietors to assemble significant experiences into client conduct. Consistently dissecting this criticism and utilizing investigation information empowers iterative upgrades to the site construction and route. The site stays in line with user expectations and industry trends thanks to a dynamic approach to refinement.

All in all, a very much created site construction and route framework are basic to making a positive client experience. Clear progressive systems, instinctive menus, responsive plan, and insightful thought of client needs by and large add to a consistent excursion through the computerized scene. By focusing on these components, site proprietors can cultivate client commitment, fulfillment, and faithfulness in a consistently advancing web-based environment.

URL Structure and Mobile Optimization

URL design and versatile improvement are basic components in making an easy to use and web crawler well disposed web-based presence. Both assume urgent parts in improving the general client experience, impacting web search tool rankings, and guaranteeing availability across different gadgets. How about we dive into every angle to figure out their importance and best practices.

URL Construction:

Not only does a well-organized URL structure help users comprehend the content hierarchy, but it also helps search engines efficiently crawl and index web pages. The following are some important things to think about when trying to improve the structure of URLs:

Comprehensibility and Pertinence:

URLs should be brief, specific, and pertinent to the content they represent.

Use dashes to isolate words, as web indexes treat them as space pointers, improving comprehensibility.

Ordered progression and Arrangement:

Coordinate URLs progressively to mirror the construction of your site. For instance, use classes and subcategories in the URL.

An unmistakable pecking order makes it more straightforward for clients and web search tools to explore through your webpage.

Stay away from Dynamic Boundaries: Limit the utilization of dynamic boundaries (e.g., meeting IDs or question strings) in URLs. Static URLs are more web search tool well disposed and client decipherable.

Canonicalization: Carry out standard labels to demonstrate the favored form of a URL, particularly while managing copy content. This assists web crawlers with uniting positioning signs.

Inclusion of Keywords: Remember significant catchphrases for URLs, yet keep away from watchword stuffing. The objective is to make a URL that is both easy to use and Website optimization cordial.

HTTPS Convention: Guarantee that your URLs utilize the safe HTTPS convention. This not only increases user trust but also plays a role in search engine rankings.

Consistency: Keep up with consistency in URL structure all through your site. Users and search engines both have an easier time comprehending the structure and seamlessly navigating it as a result of this.

Keep away from URL Boundaries for Pagination: Rather than involving URL boundaries for paginated content, consider utilizing rel="next" and rel="prev" labels in the header to show the connection between pages.

Versatile Improvement:

Optimizing your website for mobile users is crucial in light of the growing use of mobile devices. Portable streamlining guarantees a consistent and charming experience for guests getting to your site on cell phones and tablets. The following are essential

methods for efficient mobile optimization:

Responsive Plan:

Embrace a responsive website architecture that changes the format and content in view of the client's screen size. This takes out the requirement for a different portable site and guarantees a predictable encounter across gadgets.

Page Speed:

To speed up page loading, optimize images, reduce HTTP requests, and make use of browser caching. Portable clients frequently have restricted data transfer capacity, making quick stacking pages essential for a positive encounter.

Versatile Route:

Improve on route for versatile clients by utilizing a dynamic menu, simple to-tap fastens, and clear suggestions to take action. Make sure that users can easily use a single thumb to navigate your website.

Elements Suitable for Touch:

Configuration contacts agreeable components with legitimate dividing to forestall coincidental taps. On smaller screens, buttons and links should be sized appropriately and positioned for ease of use.

Enhanced Content:

Gather and focus on satisfied portable clients. Feature key data and utilize folding segments to keep pages brief while giving admittance to extra subtleties.

Versatile Enhanced Pictures and Recordings:

Pack pictures and use responsive pictures to guarantee ideal presentation on different screen sizes. Essentially, utilize dynamic video configurations to upgrade the sight and sound insight.

Viewport Design:

Set the viewport meta tag to guarantee that your site pages scale appropriately on various gadgets. This label characterizes the virtual viewport and changes the page width as needed.

Testing Across Gadgets:

Routinely test your site on various cell phones and programs to recognize and address any similarity issues. This proactive methodology guarantees a predictable encounter for all clients.

All in all, a very much organized URL and viable portable improvement are necessary parts of an effective web-based presence. By focusing on these viewpoints, you further develop web crawler perceivability as well as give a consistent and charming experience for your crowd, encouraging client commitment and fulfillment.

Page Speed and Performance

The user experience of a website is greatly influenced by page speed and performance, which affect everything from user satisfaction to search engine rankings. In the present computerized age, where capacities to focus are short and contest is wild, a sluggish stacking site can bring about disappointed clients and botched open doors.

The expression "page speed" alludes to how much time it takes for a page to stack its substance completely. This incorporates the text and pictures as well as contents, templates, and different components that add to the general usefulness and plan. Then again, "execution" incorporates a more extensive range, taking into account factors like responsiveness, intuitiveness, and the general productivity of a site.

One of the essential justifications for why page speed matters is its immediate relationship with client fulfillment. Research reliably shows that clients are bound to leave a site assuming that it takes too lengthy to even consider stacking. In this present reality where moment satisfaction is the standard, even a couple of moments of deferral can prompt a huge drop in client commitment. Sites that focus on page speed make a smoother and more pleasant experience for guests, cultivating positive impressions and empowering bring visits back.

In addition, page speed has emerged as a significant ranking factor in search engines. Page speed is one of the ranking factors that search engines, led by Google, take into account in their algorithms. Pages that load quickly are more likely to be found higher in search results, giving them a competitive advantage over slower ones. This accentuation on speed is a demonstration of the web indexes' obligation to conveying the most ideal client experience to their clients.

A few key components add to the page speed and in general execution of a site. One main consideration is the size and streamlining of pictures. Enormous, uncompressed pictures can essentially dial back a site, prompting longer burden times. By packing pictures and utilizing current picture designs, web engineers can decrease document sizes without compromising quality, working on both speed and execution.

Another vital angle is the effective utilization of contents and templates. Over the top or ineffectively advanced JavaScript and CSS documents can prevent page speed. Minifying and joining these records, as well as using non concurrent stacking whenever the situation allows, can smooth out the stacking system and upgrade by and large execution.

Optimizing page speed relies heavily on cache mechanisms. Program reserving permits much of the time to get assets to be put away locally on a client's gadget, lessening the requirement for rehashed downloads while returning to a site. Moreover, happy conveyance organizations (CDNs) appropriate site resources across numerous servers around the world, guaranteeing that clients can get to assets from the server closest to them, further improving page speed.

Portable responsiveness is one more basic figure the present computerized scene. With the rising utilization of cell phones and tablets, sites should be planned and improved for different screen sizes and gadgets. Responsive plan further develops the client experience as well as emphatically impacts web crawler rankings, as Google focuses on dynamic sites.

Page speed can be significantly affected by web hosting. Picking a solid and quick facilitating supplier is fundamental for ideal execution. Shared facilitating, while financially savvy, may prompt more slow burden times, particularly during top traffic periods. Moving up to committed or cloud facilitating can give the important assets to deal with expanded traffic and further develop by and large page speed.

Customary observing and testing are fundamental to keeping up with ideal page speed and execution. Apparatuses like Google PageSpeed Bits of knowledge and GTmetrix investigate sites, giving significant experiences into regions to progress. Nonstop testing permits web engineers to distinguish bottlenecks, address issues quickly, and guarantee a reliably smooth client experience.

All in all, page speed and execution are vital parts of an effective web-based presence. A quick stacking site upgrades client fulfillment as well as emphatically impacts web index rankings. By focusing on picture improvement, proficient prearranging and styling, reserving components, versatile responsiveness, and dependable facilitating, web designers can make a consistent and pleasant experience for clients, eventually adding to the outcome of a site in the serious computerized scene.

Chapter 3
Content Optimization

Content streamlining is a vital part of computerized promoting and online presence. Digital content is improved and refined to make it more appealing, useful, and accessible to users and search engines. From site articles and blog entries to web-based entertainment refreshes, enhancing content is vital to accomplishing better perceivability, commitment, and eventually, progress in the computerized scene.

The improvement of rankings in search engines is one of the primary objectives of content optimization. Complex algorithms are used by search engines like Google to determine the relevance and quality of content. By enhancing content, you improve the probability of your material showing up on the principal page of indexed lists, driving natural traffic to your site.

Catchphrase research is a basic move toward content improvement. It involves determining the terms and phrases that readers are most likely to use when looking for content-related information. Incorporating these catchphrases normally into your substance signs to web indexes that your material is pertinent to explicit inquiries.

Be that as it may, content streamlining goes past essentially stuffing articles with catchphrases. Quality content that is beneficial to users is given priority by search engines. In this manner, it's fundamental to make content that is useful, drawing in, and lines up with the requirements and interests of your interest group.

Organizing content for comprehensibility is one more pivotal part of improvement. Separating content into clear segments with headings, subheadings, and list items makes it all the more outwardly engaging as well as assists web search tools with grasping the construction and order of data. This upgrades the client experience, empowering guests to remain on your site longer.

Streamlining meta labels, including titles and portrayals, is fundamental for further developing navigate rates from web crawler results. A convincing title and compact, important portrayal can essentially influence a client's choice to tap on your connection. By carefully crafting these elements, you can make your content more visible and get more clicks.

Notwithstanding site design improvement (Search engine optimization), content should be customized to suit different stages and gadgets. With the rising predominance of cell phones, guaranteeing that your substance is dynamic is critical. Responsive plan, quick stacking times, and simple route add to a positive client experience, which isn't just valued by guests yet in addition leaned toward via web search tools.

Web-based entertainment assumes a critical part in satisfied circulation and perceivability. In order to optimize content for social platforms, it is necessary to comprehend the distinctive characteristics of each channel. Fitting your substance to suit the crowd and organization of explicit stages, consolidating important hashtags, and empowering social sharing can enhance your substance's compass and effect.

Routinely refreshing and reusing content is essential for a successful streamlining technique. Since new and relevant content is favored by search engines, updating your content indicates its ongoing relevance. Moreover, reusing content into various configurations, for example, infographics, recordings, or webcasts, permits you to contact a more extensive crowd and builds up your message across different channels.

Client commitment measurements, for example, bob rate, time on page, and social offers, are critical marks of content execution. Observing these measurements distinguishes regions for development and permits you to consistently refine your substance enhancement system. Breaking down client conduct empowers you to comprehend what reverberates with your crowd and change your methodology as needs be.

External link establishment is one more vital piece of content streamlining. Both inbound and outbound links improve your content's overall authority and credibility. Building quality backlinks from trustworthy sources can help your substance's remaining in web crawler rankings. Notwithstanding, it's vital for center around regular third party referencing systems and stay away from nasty or manipulative practices that can hurt your standing.

Openness is a vital thought in happy enhancement. In addition to expanding your audience, making your content accessible to people with disabilities reflects ethical and legal guidelines. This incorporates giving elective text to pictures, utilizing enlightening connection text, and planning satisfied in light of clarity.

All in all, happy improvement is a diverse methodology that joins Search engine optimization standards, client experience contemplations, and versatility to different stages. By focusing on quality, significance, and availability, you can make content that draws in web crawler consideration as well as reverberates with and connects with your main interest group. As the computerized scene keeps on developing, remaining informed about industry patterns and reliably refining your substance improvement system is fundamental for keeping a cutthroat web-based presence.

Quality Content Creation

The process of creating high-quality content is multifaceted and requires careful planning, inventiveness, and attention to detail. In the present advanced age, where data is plentiful and capacities to focus are transitory, creating content that sticks out and resounds with the crowd is essential. Whether you're a blogger, an entrepreneur, or a substance maker, understanding the vital standards of value content creation can fundamentally improve your scope and effect.

At the center of value content creation lies a profound comprehension of the main interest group. Understanding what your listeners might be thinking inclinations, interests, and trouble spots empowers you to fit your substance to address their issues. Utilizing analytics tools, extensive research, or surveys can provide useful insights into your audience's demographics and behaviors. This central information fills in as a compass, directing your substance creation endeavors in the correct course.

The fact that drives quality substance makes imaginativeness the motor. It includes breaking new ground, moving toward points from one of a kind points, and introducing data in drawing in ways. Whether you're making a blog entry, a virtual entertainment update, or a video, infusing imagination into your substance spellbinds your crowd's consideration and recognizes your image from the opposition. This could entail including elements that appeal to your audience, such as humor, storytelling, or visual appeal.

The significance of a convincing title couldn't possibly be more significant in that frame of mind of value content creation. The title fills in as the primary resource with your crowd, impacting their choice to click and draw in with your substance. A well-written headline is brief, catchy, and offers value to the reader. Techniques that can increase the impact of your headlines include employing powerful words, asking provocative questions, or instilling a sense of urgency.

Whenever you've caught your crowd's consideration, it is vital to keep up with their advantage. Your content's quality really comes through here. It's significant to follow through on the commitment made in the title by giving important, well-informed data. Whether you're creating composed content, recordings, or webcasts, guarantee that your material is useful, significant, and increases the value of your crowd's lives. This forms trust as well as lays out you as an expert in your specialty.

Consistency is a critical component in quality substance creation. Whether you're distributing day to day, week by week, or month to month, keeping a steady timetable aides construct expectation among your crowd. This unwavering quality encourages a feeling of trust, making your crowd bound to return for future substance. Consistency also applies to the tone, style, and branding of your content, resulting in a unified and recognizable brand identity.

Responsibility is a two-way street in the domain of content creation. Encourage your audience to comment, share, discuss, and interact with your content. Make opportunities for meaningful dialogue, ask questions, and respond promptly to comments. This improves the client experience as well as lifts your substance's perceivability on different stages, as numerous calculations focus on satisfied with higher commitment.

Reaching a broader audience necessitates optimizing your content for search engines. Find relevant terms and phrases that align with your content by conducting keyword research. Consolidate these catchphrases decisively in your substance, including titles, headers, and all through the body. This assists web search tools with figuring out the setting of your substance and works on its possibilities positioning higher in query items, driving natural traffic to your foundation.

Quality visuals assume a critical part in happy creation, particularly in the period of web-based entertainment. Your content will have a greater impact when you incorporate visually appealing elements, such as videos, infographics, or eye-catching images. Focus intently on making great illustrations or consider teaming up with gifted creators to raise the style of your image.

All in all, quality substance creation is a powerful cycle that requires a profound comprehension of your crowd, imagination, consistency, and vital enhancement. By focusing on these components, you can make content that catches consideration as well as constructs enduring associations with your crowd. Whether you're meaning to teach, engage, or motivate, the standards of value content creation act as a guide to progress in the steadily developing scene of computerized correspondence.

Content Relevance and Engagement

Content importance and commitment are fundamental in the present advanced scene, where a wealth of data goes after clients' consideration. Creating content that reverberates with the crowd and keeps them drew in is a diverse test that requires a profound comprehension of the interest group, vital preparation, and dynamic variation to developing patterns.

At the center of content pertinence is the arrangement between what the crowd looks for and what the substance conveys. Distinguishing and grasping the necessities, inclinations, and ways of behaving of the interest group is the most vital phase in making pertinent substance. This includes statistical surveying, investigation, and persistent observing of crowd input. By utilizing these bits of knowledge, content makers can fit their material to address explicit trouble spots, wants, or interests, guaranteeing that it measures up to the crowd's assumptions.

Significance is definitely not a static idea yet a powerful one that develops with time and evolving patterns. Remaining sensitive to industry advancements, social moves, and arising themes is critical for keeping up with content pertinence. Pattern examination devices, social listening stages, and normal crowd reviews can be significant assets in this continuous cycle. Creators can connect with their audience and establish themselves as trustworthy sources of current information by adapting their content to reflect current interests and concerns.

Relevant content should be contextually appropriate for the platform and medium through which it is delivered in addition to meeting audience expectations. Figuring out the subtleties of every stage - whether it's a blog, web-based entertainment channel, web recording, or video stage - is fundamental. Fitting substance to suit the organization and assumptions for the picked medium upgrades its perceivability and availability, improving the probability of commitment.

Commitment, the second mainstay of effective substance, is tied in with making a two-way collaboration between the substance maker and the crowd. It is more than just passive consumption; It entails encouraging user participation in the form of comments, likes, and shares. This communication upgrades the client experience as well as signs to calculations that the substance is significant and deserving of advancement.

One vital part of cultivating commitment is to construct a local area around the substance. Laying out a feeling of having a place and divided interest between the crowd empowers dynamic investment. Content makers can accomplish this by answering remarks, facilitating live meetings, and making client produced content missions. When the audience feels valued and heard, they are more likely to pay attention to the content and give it their time.

One more basic component of commitment is narrating. People are wired to answer stories, and meshing accounts into content can enrapture the crowd's feelings and creative mind. Whether it's an individual tale, a contextual investigation, or a made up situation, narrating adds a layer of association that rises above simple data conveyance. The content can be remembered and shared because of this emotional engagement, which can have a lasting effect.

Moreover, intuitive components like surveys, tests, and reviews can transform inactive purchasers into dynamic members. By welcoming the crowd to offer their viewpoints or test their insight, makers upgrade commitment as well as accumulate important bits of knowledge into crowd inclinations and ways of behaving.

Finding some kind of harmony among pertinence and commitment includes nonstop refinement and enhancement. Dissecting execution measurements, for example, navigate rates, bob rates, and virtual entertainment examination, gives important input on what works and what needs change. Content creators can improve their strategies, fine-tune their targeting, and optimize their content with a data-driven approach.

All in all, satisfied significance and commitment are entwined points of support that structure the underpinning of fruitful advanced correspondence. In addition to a commitment to remaining up to date with current trends, creating content that resonates with the audience necessitates a comprehensive comprehension of their requirements and preferences. Fostering engagement requires creating a dynamic and interactive experience that goes beyond merely consumption once relevance has been established. By ceaselessly refining methodologies in light of information driven bits of knowledge, content makers can construct and support a dedicated crowd in the consistently developing computerized scene.

Multimedia Integration

Sight and sound coordination is a dynamic and developing field that includes joining different types of media to make a durable and intuitive experience. As innovation propels, the consistent combination of text, illustrations, sound, video, and intelligent components turns out to be progressively significant in different applications, going from website composition and advertising to schooling and diversion.

One critical part of sight and sound reconciliation is the cooperative energy between various media types. By mixing text with visuals, for example, pictures or designs, data can be conveyed all the more really. This integration improves the user experience as a whole and caters to various learning styles. For instance, a site with media components can catch the consideration of guests more really than a plain text page, prompting expanded commitment and understanding.

Multimedia content is further enhanced by the incorporation of audio and video components. Sites, introductions, and instructive materials frequently consolidate recordings to convey data in a really captivating and important way. Sound can be used in conjunction with visuals to create a multisensory experience that engages the audience.

This coordination is especially obvious in fields like e-realizing, where intelligent media content upgrades the viability of instructive materials.

Intelligent sight and sound takes combination to a higher level by permitting clients to draw in with the substance effectively. This can incorporate intelligent illustrations, reenactments, and computer generated reality encounters. These kinds of applications are common in industries like gaming, where players become a part of the multimedia environment and have an impact on the story or outcome. Intelligent media is likewise broadly utilized in preparing reenactments, giving sensible situations to students to rehearse and refine their abilities.

In the domain of web improvement, mixed media joining assumes a critical part in making outwardly engaging and easy to understand sites. Integrating pictures, recordings, and intelligent components upgrades the style as well as further develops the general client experience. This is urgent for holding guests and passing on data effectively. With the ascent of responsive plan, mixed media components should adjust consistently to various gadgets and screen sizes, highlighting the significance of insightful combination.

Multimedia integration is an effective strategy for delivering brand messages and attracting customers' attention in advertising and marketing. Joining text, pictures, and recordings in missions can make a convincing story that resounds with the interest group. Virtual entertainment stages, specifically, influence sight and sound combination to work with commitment and virality, as clients are bound to share content that incorporates a blend of media types.

Interactive media combination is additionally changing the field of news coverage. Conventional media sources are integrating recordings, intelligent designs, and digital broadcasts to improve narrating and give a more vivid news experience. This shift answers changing buyer inclinations, as crowds progressively look for mixed media rich substance that conveys data in a seriously captivating and edible configuration.

The difficulties in mixed media joining incorporate guaranteeing similarity across various stages and gadgets. Engineers should consider changing screen sizes, goals, and handling capacities to convey a predictable encounter. Furthermore, there are concerns connected with availability, as sight and sound substances might give boundaries for people's incapacities. Endeavors to address these difficulties include utilizing responsive plan standards, improving interactive media resources, and sticking to openness norms.

Looking forward, the development of media combination is intently attached to headways in innovation. Arising advancements like increased reality (AR) and augmented reality (VR) present additional opportunities for vivid mixed media encounters. In particular, augmented reality (AR) has the potential to create interactive and context-aware multimedia applications by overlaying digital data on the real world.

All in all, sight and sound mix is a dynamic and extraordinary power across different fields. Whether in training, amusement, advertising, or news coverage, the collaboration of text, illustrations, sound, video, and intelligent components upgrades correspondence and commitment. As innovation keeps on propelling, the consistent mix of different media types will assume a focal part in forming the fate of computerized encounters.

Chapter 4
User Experience (UX) and SEO

Client Experience (UX) and Site improvement (Search engine optimization) are two basic parts that essentially influence a site's prosperity. While they fill particular needs, their interchange is urgent for accomplishing ideal web-based execution. Let's investigate the intricate relationship that exists between SEO and user experience and see how they can coexist in harmony.

Understanding Client Experience (UX):

Client Experience alludes to the general experience a client has while collaborating with a site or application. It envelops different viewpoints, including plan, ease of use, openness, and generally fulfillment. Visitors who have a positive user experience are more likely to successfully accomplish their objectives, locate relevant information, and navigate the site.

A user-centered approach is essential in UX. Sites that focus on client necessities and inclinations will quite often make a more pleasant and connecting experience. Components, for example, instinctive route, clear source of inspiration buttons, and responsive plan add to a positive UX.

The Web optimization Association:

Site improvement, then again, spins around methodologies and procedures to upgrade a site's perceivability in web search tool results. Website design enhancement intends to upgrade different elements, including watchwords, content quality, and backlinks, to further develop a webpage's positioning. The ultimate objective is to boost conversion rates and attract organic traffic.

The association among UX and Web optimization lies in the way that web search tools, especially Google, consider client experience as a vital positioning component. Google's calculations are intended to focus on sites that give a positive and pertinent experience for clients. This implies that a site with a superior UX is probably going to rank higher in query items, in a roundabout way impacting its Website optimization execution.

Important Intersectional Zones:
Page Speed:

The loading speed of a website has an impact on both UX and SEO. Slow-stacking pages disappoint clients as well as lead to higher bob rates, adversely affecting UX. According to a Web optimization point of view, Google considers page speed as a positioning element, underlining the significance of a quick and proficient site.

Versatile Plan:

Mobile-friendliness is essential for both user experience and search engine optimization (SEO). The user experience on mobile devices is enhanced by a responsive design that adjusts to a variety of screen sizes. Also, Google focuses on dynamic sites in its versatile list items, building up the significance of portable improvement for Website design enhancement.

Content Quality:

Top caliber, pertinent substance is a foundation for both UX and Website optimization. Websites that provide useful information are rewarded by search engines because users look for it. Making content that tends to client plan, consolidates important catchphrases, and is very much organized adds to a positive client experience while supporting Search engine optimization execution.

Metrics for User Engagement:

Measurements, for example, skip rate, time nearby, and active visitor clicking percentage are characteristic of client commitment and fulfillment. Web indexes utilize these measurements to assess the importance and nature of a site's substance. A site with high client commitment is bound to rank higher in query items, overcoming any barrier among UX and Search engine optimization.

Techniques for Collaboration:
Watchword Exploration and Client Aim:

Adjusting watchword procedures to client goal is fundamental. By understanding what clients are looking for, you can make content that fulfills their necessities. This upgrades the general client experience as well as works on the pertinence of your substance according to web search tools.

Structure of the Site Optimized:

A site's structure that is well-organized makes it easier for users to navigate and for search engines to crawl. Coherent and natural route further develops UX, while an unmistakable site structure assists web search tools with grasping the order and significance of various pages.

Responsive Plan:

Embracing a responsive plan guarantees that your site gives a consistent encounter across different gadgets. This advantages clients as well as lines up with Google's inclination for versatile destinations, decidedly influencing Website design enhancement.

Page Stacking Velocity:

Focus on upgrading page stacking velocity to make a smoother client experience. Quicker stacking pages lessen skip rates as well as add to higher web index rankings.

The symbiotic relationship that exists between User Experience and Search Engine Optimization cannot be denied in the ever-evolving digital landscape. A client driven approach upgrades the fulfillment of site guests as well as lines up with the measures that web search tools use to decide rankings.

By perceiving the interconnectedness of UX and Search engine optimization, site proprietors and advertisers can foster methodologies that make an agreeable equilibrium, at last prompting further developed perceivability, expanded traffic, and higher transformation rates. Embracing this collaboration isn't simply a best practice; it is a need in the cutthroat web-based climate where achievement relies on gathering client assumptions and web crawler prerequisites all the while.

Importance of UX in Search Rankings

The significance of Client Experience (UX) in search rankings couldn't possibly be more significant in the unique scene of computerized promoting. As web search tools constantly develop, focusing on client driven factors has turned into a critical determinant in a site's perceivability and achievement. The collaboration among UX and search rankings goes past feel, diving into the domain of client fulfillment, commitment, and generally speaking site execution.

At its center, web crawlers expect to furnish clients with the most important and significant data because of their questions. As search calculations become progressively complex, they center around watchword importance as well as on the general experience clients have on a site. Google, the main web search tool, has unequivocally underlined the significance of client experience as a positioning element through refreshes like Center Web Vitals.

Page speed is an important factor in UX that affects search engine rankings. Web indexes focus on sites that heap rapidly, perceiving that a consistent and quick client experience adds to higher fulfillment. Slow-stacking pages disappoint clients as well as result in higher bob rates, adversely affecting a site's hunt positioning. Enhancement of pictures, utilizing program storing, and limiting server reaction time are vital stages in upgrading page speed and, thus, further developing pursuit rankings.

Portable responsiveness is one more essential component in the UX and search rankings condition. With the rising commonness of cell phone utilization, web indexes focus on versatile sites. Google's portable first ordering implies that the versatile rendition of a site is viewed as the essential hotspot for ordering and positioning. Sites that offer a smooth, responsive experience across different gadgets are bound to rank higher in query items, mirroring the web search tools' obligation to conveying a positive client experience.

User experience and, by extension, search engine rankings are significantly influenced by a website's structure and navigability. An efficient site with route ways guarantees that clients can undoubtedly find the data they look for. Websites with intuitive structures are given higher priority in search results by search engines. Executing easy to use route improves Website design enhancement as well as keeps guests drawn in, lessening bob rates and indicating to web search tools that the substance is important.

Content importance and quality are basic to both client experience and search rankings. The likelihood of a user remaining engaged for an extended period of time is increased by websites whose content is well-crafted and informative. Web crawlers assess content profundity, significance, and uniqueness, remunerating sites that reliably convey important data. It is still essential for SEO to naturally incorporate keywords into high-quality content because doing so strikes a balance between optimizing for search engines and providing users with useful information.

The meaning of client commitment measurements in search rankings can't be overlooked. Measurements like active visitor clicking percentage (CTR), stay time, and skip rate furnish experiences into how clients communicate with a site. Higher CTRs and longer stay times sign to web search tools that clients see as the substance important and locking in. On the other hand, a high bounce rate may indicate that the content provided does not meet user expectations. By breaking down these measurements, web indexes survey the general client experience and change rankings as needs be.

Client trust is an elusive yet powerful method to calculate the domain of UX and search rankings. Users and search engines alike are more likely to favor trustworthy websites. Factors like secure HTTPS associations, straightforward protection strategies, and tenable backlinks add to building trust. Google, specifically, values site security and utilizes it as a positioning element. Trust is cultivated and search rankings are improved when user data protection and online security are prioritized.

Social signs, while not immediate positioning elements, are firmly connected to client experience. Online entertainment stages are strong channels for content appropriation and commitment. By expanding their online presence, websites that encourage social sharing and interaction may indirectly influence search rankings. The connection between friendly signals and search rankings highlights the interconnectedness of client experience across different computerized touchpoints.

Taking everything into account, the interaction among UX and search rankings is complicated and complex. Focusing on client experience goes past a simple journey for tasteful allure; it straightforwardly influences a site's perceivability, commitment, and believability according to the two clients and web indexes. As calculations keep on developing, understanding and adjusting to the advancing scene of UX becomes central for organizations and computerized advertisers meaning to get and keep an upper hand in the web-based space.

Navigation and Accessibility

Route and openness assume critical parts in guaranteeing that computerized stages, sites, and applications are easy to understand and comprehensive for all people, no matter what their capacities or handicaps. In the quick moving computerized period, where data is bountiful and innovation is universal, making an available and traversable advanced space is foremost.

Navigation: Effective route is the foundation of a positive client experience. It includes the game plan of data and elements in a manner that permits clients to effectively find what they are searching for. Instinctive route improves client commitment and fulfillment, adding to the general outcome of a computerized item.

Various leveled Design: A very much planned progressive construction puts together data in a sensible way, working with a consistent route. This includes sorting content into fundamental segments, sub-areas, and pages. Users ought to be able to effortlessly navigate through the various sections and comprehend the connections that exist between them.

Detailed Descriptions and Labels: Another important part of navigation is labeling. Clear and succinct marks for buttons, connections, and menus added to a comprehension client might interpret the point of interaction. Clear text gives setting and helps clients in settling on informed conclusions about where to explore straightaway.

Responsive Plan: In the time of assorted gadgets and screen sizes, responsive plan guarantees that route stays viable across different stages. A responsive point of interaction adjusts to various screen sizes, keeping up with ease of use and openness whether clients access the advanced space from a personal computer, tablet, or cell phone.

Accessibility: On the other hand, accessibility focuses on making sure that everyone, including people with disabilities, can access and use digital content. It goes past the plan and format, incorporating different components to establish a comprehensive climate.

Screen Peruser Similarity: Screen readers are essential devices that transform digital text into synthesized speech for people who are blind or visually impaired. Guaranteeing similarity with screen perusers includes giving elective text to pictures, depicting the substance and usefulness of components, and sorting out data such that seems OK when perused resoundingly.

Console Route: Not all clients can depend on a mouse or contact screen for route. Console route is a major part of openness, permitting clients to explore through a site or application utilizing just the console. This is especially significant for people with engine incapacities who might experience issues utilizing a mouse.

Variety Difference and Visual Plan: Thought of variety contrast is essential for clients with visual hindrances or partial blindness. Content is eligible for all users when there is sufficient contrast between text and background. Moreover, a reasonable and steady visual plan helps clients with mental disabilities by diminishing disarray and further developing understanding.

Subtitling and Records: Media content, like recordings and digital broadcasts, ought to be joined by inscriptions or records. This advantages clients with hearing debilitations and guarantees that data is available in various configurations. Giving options to simply sound or visual substance is a vital standard of comprehensive plan.

Versatile Innovations: The digital landscape and adaptive technologies should both continue to change. This remembers progressions for assistive advancements, for example, voice acknowledgment, eye-GPS beacons, and haptic criticism interfaces. Keeping up with these advancements enables developers and designers to incorporate the most recent accessibility-enhancing tools.

The Convergence of Route and Availability:

In the quest for an accessible digital experience, the synergy between navigation and accessibility is evident. A very much explored site or application that embraces openness standards turns into an inviting space for clients, everything being equal.

Client Testing and Input: Ceaseless client testing and criticism circles are fundamental for refining both route and openness highlights. Utilizing individuals with a variety of abilities to conduct usability tests provides valuable insights into potential areas for improvement. Client input, whether from people with disabilities or everyone, guides iterative plan processes.

Legal and moral obligations: Past client experience, there are lawful and moral objectives for focusing on openness. Numerous nations have executed guidelines and norms, for example, the Internet Content Availability Rules (WCAG), to guarantee that advanced stages comply with openness standards. Sticking to these norms assists associations with conforming to lawful prerequisites as well as lines up with moral practices.

All in all, route and openness are entwined components that characterize the client experience in the computerized domain. A very much organized route framework upgrades convenience, while openness guarantees that this ease of use stretches out to a different client base.

An environment in which digital spaces are accessible to all, regardless of physical or cognitive abilities, is created by striking a balance between inclusive design and intuitive navigation. Not only does this commitment to inclusivity meet legal requirements, but it also demonstrates a commitment to making the digital world truly accessible to everyone.

Responsive Design

Responsive plan is an essential part of present day web improvement, meaning to give clients a consistent and ideal survey insight across different gadgets and screen sizes. As the advanced scene keeps on developing, the requirement for sites to adjust to various stages has become progressively basic. This flexibility is unequivocally what responsive plan addresses.

At its center, responsive planning is a way to deal with website composition that makes site pages render well on various gadgets and window or screen sizes. A consistent user experience can be achieved by making use of images, CSS media queries, and flexible grids and layouts. The essential objective is to guarantee that a similar substance is open and outwardly engaging, whether or not it is seen on a personal computer, PC, tablet, or cell phone.

One of the critical parts of a responsive plan is liquid matrices. Customary website architecture frequently depends on fixed-width designs, which can cause issues when seen on various gadgets. Responsive plan uses relative units like rates rather than fixed units like pixels, permitting content to powerfully conform to the screen size. This guarantees that the design stays relative, giving a more amicable client experience.

Another critical component is adaptable pictures. Pictures assume a huge part in website architecture, however they can be a wellspring of disappointment with regards to responsive designs. By using CSS to make images scale with the size of the screen, responsive design addresses this issue and prevents them from breaking the layout or going beyond the viewport. This guarantees that pictures are outwardly satisfying as well as improve the general responsiveness of the plan.

Responsive design relies on media queries as its foundation. They permit engineers to apply explicit styles for various gadgets or screen sizes. Developers can use media queries to set breakpoints where the layout needs to change to fit different screen sizes. This adaptability considers a custom fitted client experience, enhancing the plan for every gadget without the requirement for independent sites or applications.

Responsive plan isn't just about feel; it additionally fundamentally influences client commitment and site design improvement (Website optimization). Google, the prevailing web crawler, thinks about versatility as a positioning element. Sites that are not dynamic might encounter lower search rankings, influencing their perceivability to clients. Responsive plan guarantees that a site is open and easy to understand across all gadgets, adding to better Search engine optimization execution.

Besides, in a period where portable utilization has outperformed work area use, taking care of versatile clients isn't simply a decision however a need. Responsive plan empowers sites to contact a more extensive crowd, obliging the different ways individuals access data. Whether clients are in a hurry with their cell phones or sitting at a work area with a PC, a responsive plan guarantees a steady and pleasant experience.

Online business is one area where a responsive plan is especially essential. With the ascent of versatile shopping, online retailers should give a consistent and instinctive experience for clients making buys on different gadgets. A responsive plan approach permits online business sites to streamline item shows, route, and checkout processes, cultivating a positive shopping experience and possibly expanding transformation rates.

The advancement of web improvement systems and apparatuses has additionally worked with the execution of responsive plans. Structures like Bootstrap and Establishment give engineers a bunch of pre-planned parts and a responsive framework, smoothing out the most common way of making responsive sites. These systems save time as well as stick to best works, guaranteeing a hearty and very much tried starting point for responsive plans.

All in all, responsive planning is a key part of present day web improvement, tending to the different ways clients access content. It affects user experience, SEO, and a website's overall success beyond aesthetics. As innovation keeps on progressing, responsive planning will stay a basic methodology, empowering sites to adjust and flourish in a constantly changing computerized scene.

Chapter 5
Local SEO

Neighborhood Website design enhancement, or nearby site

improvement, is an urgent part of computerized showcasing that spotlights on streamlining a business' internet based presence to draw in nearby clients. For small businesses, brick-and-mortar stores, and service providers, mastering local SEO is essential in an era when consumers increasingly rely on search engines to locate local businesses.

Significance of Neighborhood Search engine optimization

1. Expanded Perceivability:

A company's visibility in local search results is improved by local SEO. At the point when potential clients look for items or administrations in their area, organizations that have enhanced their web-based presence are bound to show up conspicuously in web search tool results pages (SERPs).

2. Versatile Hunt Strength:

With the ascent of cell phones, nearby hunts have become more common. Purchasers frequently look for organizations "close to me" utilizing their cell phones. Local SEO ensures that businesses are optimized for mobile searches, making it simpler for customers to locate them and communicate with them while they are on the go.

3. Upper hand:

For neighborhood organizations, particularly those with actual areas, nearby Website design enhancement gives an upper hand. At the point when shoppers are given various choices, organizations that show up at the highest point of nearby query items are bound to catch their consideration and, subsequently, their business.

Key Components of Neighborhood Search engine optimization

1. Google My Business (GMB):

One of the foundations of nearby Website optimization is making and enhancing a Google My Professional reference. This free instrument from Google permits organizations to give fundamental data, for example, address, telephone number, business hours, and audits. A very much improved GMB profile essentially helps a business' possibilities showing up in nearby guide packs and natural query items.

2. Nearby Catchphrases:

Consolidating area explicit catchphrases in site content, meta labels, and different components assists web crawlers with grasping the geographic significance of a business. This improves the probability of the business showing up in nearby hunt questions.

3. Online Audits:

Client surveys assume an urgent part in neighborhood Search engine optimization. Positive surveys improve a business' standing as well as add to higher rankings in nearby list items. Empowering fulfilled clients to leave surveys on stages like Google, Howl, and other industry-explicit audit destinations is an important neighborhood Search engine optimization methodology.

4. Nearby References:

Steady business data across online catalogs and reference destinations is essential for nearby Website design enhancement. Precise and state-of-the-art references, including Rest (Name, Address, Telephone number) subtleties, indicate to web search tools that a business is genuine and dependable.

5. Localization of the Website:
Improving a business' site for neighborhood search incorporates making area explicit greeting pages, remembering nearby catchphrases for meta labels, and it is versatile to guarantee that the site. This assists web search tools with grasping the pertinence of the business to neighborhood clients.

Techniques for Neighborhood Website optimization Achievement

1. Study of Keywords:
Lead exhaustive watchword exploration to recognize the most important and much of the time looked through terms connected with your business and area. This structures the establishment for making content and upgrading on the web resources.

2. Confined Content:
Foster substance that takes care of the neighborhood crowd. This might entail writing blog posts, articles, or other kinds of content that draw attention to local happenings, news, or trends. This draws in nearby guests as well as signs to web crawlers that the business is profoundly associated with the local area.

3. Versatile Improvement:
Given the commonness of portable quests in neighborhood settings, guaranteeing that your site is versatile is principal. Google's versatile first ordering focuses on dynamic sites, making it a vital component for nearby Web optimization achievement.

4. Building links:

Construct neighborhood backlinks from trustworthy sites inside your local area or industry. These backlinks sign to web crawlers that your business is a trusted and definitive source inside the nearby setting.

5. Web-based Entertainment Presence:

Influence online entertainment stages to draw in with the neighborhood local area. Standard updates, advancements, and local area inclusion exhibited via virtual entertainment add to a positive internet based presence, influencing neighborhood search rankings.

Estimating Nearby Website optimization Achievement

1. Google Investigation:

Use Google Examination to follow site traffic, client conduct, and transformations. By putting forth unambiguous objectives and following applicable measurements, organizations can survey the effect of their neighborhood Website design enhancement endeavors on internet based execution.

2. GMB Statistics:

Screen Google My Business bits of knowledge to follow how clients track down your business, where they are found, and what moves they initiate. This information gives significant experiences into the adequacy of your neighborhood Search engine optimization technique.

3. Positioning Reports:

Consistently check your business' rankings in nearby list items. Apparatuses like Moz, SEMrush, and neighborhood rank following programming can give point by point providing details regarding watchword rankings and perceivability in nearby ventures.

All in all, neighborhood Search engine optimization is irreplaceable for organizations meaning to flourish in their nearby business sectors. By improving web-based resources, drawing in with the nearby local area, and keeping up to date with calculation refreshes, organizations can upgrade their perceivability, draw in additional clients, and lay out areas of strength for an in their neighborhood markets.

Importance of Local Search

Neighborhood search is a basic part of online perceivability and business outcome in the present computerized age. As buyers progressively go to the web to find items and administrations, the significance of nearby inquiry couldn't possibly be more significant. An amazing asset associates organizations with their interest group in a particular geographic area, making it a foundation of showcasing systems for nearby organizations.

One of the essential reasons neighborhood search is vital is its effect on purchaser conduct. People frequently use location-specific terms like "near me" or city names when searching for products or services. This pattern has been energized by the pervasiveness of cell phones, empowering clients to look in a hurry and get significant, area based results. Optimized for local search, businesses have a better chance of being found by potential customers actively searching for what they offer in a specific area.

Besides, neighborhood search is intently attached to the ascent of voice search. With the developing ubiquity of remote helpers and savvy speakers, clients are progressively depending on voice orders to track down data. Voice look frequently have a neighborhood aim, as clients ask about neighboring organizations or administrations. For organizations, this stresses the need to advance their web-based presence for voice search, guaranteeing that they are effectively discoverable through voice-actuated gadgets.

The effect of neighborhood search stretches out past web-based perceivability; it straightforwardly impacts people walking through to actual stores. A significant proportion of local searches result in in-store visits within a day, according to studies. This underlines the basic job neighborhood search plays in driving disconnected transformations. Organizations that focus on neighborhood inquiry improvement draw in web-based clients as well as improve the probability of drawing in people strolling through to their physical areas.

Additionally, the significance of nearby pursuit is clear in its effect on shopper trust. Numerous customers depend on internet based audits and evaluations to arrive at informed conclusions about which organizations to disparage. Nearby query items frequently show these surveys, and organizations with positive input are bound to procure the trust of expected clients. On the other hand, organizations disregarding their internet based standing might miss out on business amazing open doors, as bad audits can prevent forthcoming clients from picking their administrations.

Nearby site design improvement (Website optimization) is a key methodology for organizations hoping to saddle the force of neighborhood search. This involves making a website's content, meta tags, and business listings more relevant to local searches by optimizing them. Furthermore, guaranteeing and improving a Google My Professional reference is a significant stage, as it guarantees exact business data is shown in neighborhood list items, including address, telephone number, and business hours.

Local search is important for more than just small businesses; indeed, even huge endeavors with a worldwide presence perceive its importance. Numerous worldwide brands have embraced hyper-restricted advertising techniques, fitting their missions to resound with explicit neighborhood crowds. This approach permits them to lay out a more special interaction with shoppers in various districts, cultivating brand steadfastness and importance.

For businesses of all sizes, local search is also a cost-effective marketing tool. Contrasted with customary publicizing strategies, for example, print or TV promotions, neighborhood inquiry enhancement can give a better yield on venture. It permits organizations to target explicit socioeconomics and geological regions, arriving at expected clients at the right second when they are effectively looking for pertinent items or administrations.

All in all, the significance of nearby pursuit in the computerized scene couldn't possibly be more significant. A dynamic and persuasive power shapes customer conduct, drives people walking through, forms trust, and gives a savvy showcasing road for organizations. As innovation keeps on developing, organizations that focus on neighborhood inquiry streamlining will stay strategically set up to flourish in the serious web-based commercial center, interfacing with their nearby crowd and receiving the rewards of major areas of strength for a noticeable internet based presence.

Google My Business Optimization

Google My Business (GMB) improvement is a critical part of any neighborhood business' internet based presence. With north of 5 billion hunts occurring on Google every day, it's fundamental for organizations to use GMB to improve their perceivability and draw in expected clients.

As a matter of some importance, guaranteeing and checking your business on Google My Business is the underlying step. This lays out your web-based presence as well as guarantees that you have command over the data shown about your business on Google. Giving precise and exceptional data, for example, your business name, address, telephone number, site, and business hours is significant. This data assists clients with tracking down your business as well as adds to how research might interpret your business, working on its possibilities appearing in applicable neighborhood look.

Enhancing your business portrayal is one more key variable in GMB streamlining. Create a convincing and succinct depiction that plainly imparts what your business offers. Incorporate pertinent watchwords that potential clients could utilize while looking for items or administrations like yours. This not just further develops your GMB posting's web crawler perceivability yet in addition gives important data to possible clients.

The attributes feature in GMB is a straightforward yet efficient method for providing additional information about your company. Whether it's featuring conveniences, administrations, or novel selling focuses, adding qualities can make your posting more enlightening and engaging. This can be especially gainful for organizations in serious business sectors, helping them stick out and draw in the right crowd.

Review management is an essential part of GMB optimization because customer reviews have a significant impact on potential customers. Positive reviews from satisfied customers should be encouraged, and negative reviews should be promptly addressed in a polite and solution-oriented manner. Drawing in with client audits constructs entrust with your crowd as well as signs to find out that you are a functioning and client driven business.

Photographs are a useful asset in GMB enhancement. Organizations with photographs get 42% more demands for headings and 35% more snap throughs to their sites. Guarantee that your GMB posting has top notch pictures displaying your items, administrations, group, and the general environment of your business. Routinely refreshing your photograph exhibition can keep your posting new and drawing in for expected clients.

Posts on Google My Business give a powerful method for sharing updates, advancements, occasions, and other important data straightforwardly on your posting. These posts show up in your business profile and in neighborhood query items, making them a compelling method for speaking with your crowd. Posting updates on a regular basis keeps your company's information up to date and encourages customer engagement.

Developing nearby references is indispensable for GMB improvement. These are online notices of your business' name, address, and telephone number (Rest) on outer sites, catalogs, and social stages. Consistency in Rest data across the web assembles entrust with the two clients and web crawlers, emphatically affecting your neighborhood search rankings.

By making use of Google My Business Insights, you can get useful statistics about how well your listing is doing. This remembers information for how clients track down your business, where they're found, and the moves they initiate on your GMB posting. Breaking down this information can assist you with pursuing informed choices to additionally enhance your posting and design your techniques to all the more likely arrive at your ideal interest group.

Executing a nearby Website design enhancement technique close by GMB streamlining is a strong mix. This includes streamlining your site for nearby catchphrases, making area based content, and building excellent backlinks from neighborhood sources. A solid neighborhood Website design enhancement technique supplements GMB improvement, assisting your business with positioning higher in nearby query items.

All in all, Google My Business enhancement is a multi-layered technique that includes guaranteeing and checking your posting, giving precise data, streamlining your business depiction, using credits, overseeing client surveys, displaying excellent photographs, consistently posting refreshes, developing neighborhood references, and examining bits of knowledge. By putting time and exertion into GMB streamlining, organizations can improve their web-based perceivability, draw in additional clients, and remain serious in the nearby market.

Local Citations and Reviews

Neighborhood references and surveys assume a critical part in forming the web-based presence and notoriety of organizations. In the computerized age, where customers vigorously depend on the web to settle on informed choices, these components essentially influence an organization's perceivability, validity, and at last, its prosperity.

Nearby References:

Neighborhood references allude to online notices of a business' name, address, and telephone number (Rest) across different stages like professional listings, virtual entertainment, and nearby sites. These references act as a virtual unique mark, giving consistency and authenticity to a business' data across the web. Web crawlers like Google utilize these references to confirm the precision of business subtleties, affecting nearby pursuit rankings.

For organizations intending to improve their neighborhood Website design enhancement (Website streamlining), keeping up with precise and state-of-the-art references is fundamental. Conflicting data can prompt disarray among both web crawlers and likely clients, possibly bringing about lower search rankings and botched business open doors.

Besides, neighborhood references add to the foundation of a business' internet based power. At the point when an organization is reliably referenced across trustworthy stages, it signs to web search tools that the business is pertinent and dependable. As a result, its chances of appearing in local search results increase.

To actually oversee neighborhood references, organizations ought to guarantee their Rest data is steady across all stages, routinely update their subtleties, and look for consideration in applicable nearby registries. Moreover, observing and remedying any mistakes instantly is significant for keeping a positive web-based presence.

Reviews:

Client surveys are strong powerhouses that can influence possible clients' perspectives and drive their buying choices. Positive surveys go about as tributes, building trust and validity for a business, while negative surveys can unfavorably affect its standing. Subsequently, overseeing and utilizing web surveys is a critical part of online standing administration.

Organizations ought to effectively urge fulfilled clients to leave positive surveys, as these act as an important type of social evidence. A company's visibility in search results is enhanced by positive reviews, which not only attract potential customers but also make a positive contribution to the algorithms of search engines.

In any case, negative surveys are unavoidable, and the way that a business handles them can be similarly significant. Responsiveness is critical; tending to negative input expeditiously and expertly can show a promise to consumer loyalty. In addition, potential customers frequently have a positive impression of businesses when they see efforts to address issues and improve based on feedback.

Organizations can effectively draw in with surveys by answering both positive and negative criticism. Offering thanks for positive surveys shows appreciation for client service, while tending to worries in bad audits exhibits responsibility and a pledge to constant improvement.

The effect of online audits stretches out past pursuit rankings and client trust; they likewise impact nearby pack rankings. The set of business listings that are prominently accompanied by maps on search engine results pages is known as the local pack. Businesses with more positive reviews are more likely to show up in the local pack, making them more visible to potential clients.

Reviews are no longer restricted to specific review platforms in this day and age of social media and user-generated content. Virtual entertainment stages like Facebook, Howl, and Google My Business are normal spaces for clients to share their encounters. In this way, organizations ought to effectively screen and draw in with surveys on different stages to keep a positive web-based presence.

All in all, nearby references and surveys are fundamental parts of a business' web-based presence. Steady and precise nearby references improve a business' perceivability in neighborhood look, while positive surveys fabricate trust and believability among expected clients. Effectively dealing with these components is fundamental for organizations hoping to flourish in the serious computerized scene, as they straightforwardly influence search rankings, client discernments, and generally achievement.

Chapter 6
SEO Analytics and Measurement

Website design enhancement examination and estimation assume a critical part in the outcome of any web-based presence. Understanding and making use of the insights provided by SEO analytics become increasingly important as businesses strive to increase their visibility in search engines. This comprehensive strategy involves tracking, analyzing, and interpreting data in order to make well-informed decisions that increase website performance and organic traffic.

Keyword analysis is an important part of SEO analytics. To reach your target audience, you must choose the right keywords. Devices like Google Examination, SEMrush, and Ahrefs help in finding pertinent catchphrases, surveying their pursuit volume, and assessing the opposition. This information permits organizations to streamline their substance with watchwords that can possibly rank well and reverberate with their crowd.

Whenever catchphrases are chosen, checking rankings becomes basic. Following watchword positions over the long run gives bits of knowledge into the adequacy of Website design enhancement methodologies. A steady move in rankings shows positive improvement endeavors, while a decay might connote the requirement for changes. Standard position empowers organizations to adjust their substance and backlink systems to keep up with or advance their situations in web search tool results pages (SERPs).

Past watchword examination, Search engine optimization investigation incorporate on-page measurements that assess the exhibition of individual pages. Measurements like page load speed, skip rate, and time on page straightforwardly influence client experience and web search tool rankings. A sluggish stacking page or high bob rate might flag issues that need consideration, for example, streamlining pictures, further developing server reaction times, or improving substance significance.

Backlink examination is one more pivotal part of Search engine optimization estimation. Backlinks, or approaching connections from different sites, contribute fundamentally to web search tool calculations. Apparatuses like Moz and Lofty assist in evaluating the quality and amount of backlinks. Observing the development of backlinks, distinguishing respectable sources, and tending to poisonous connections are crucial for keeping a solid connection profile and upgrading web index trust.

Site traffic examination remains closely connected with Website optimization estimation. Insights are gained by analyzing traffic sources, user demographics, and user behavior. Natural traffic, driven by Search engine optimization endeavors, ought to be an essential concentration. Furthermore, understanding how clients explore the site, which pages they visit, and how lengthy they stay helps in refining content and further developing in general site structure.

SEO analytics' ultimate goal is conversion tracking. Transformations can shift from finishing a buy to finishing up a contact structure. Google Examination and other investigation stages empower organizations to set up change following, permitting them to quantify the adequacy of their Search engine optimization procedures in producing wanted activities. By crediting transformations to explicit catchphrases or pages, organizations can refine their way to deal with boost results.

Nearby Website design enhancement examinations are fundamental for organizations focusing on a particular geographic region. Upgrading for neighborhood search includes overseeing professional references, gathering client surveys, and guaranteeing precise Rest (Name, Address, n. N. Telephone number) data. Apparatuses like Google My Business and nearby Website optimization review devices assist organizations with observing their neighborhood online presence and address any irregularities or issues.

Ordinary Website optimization reviews are a proactive measure to recognize and redress expected issues. Reviews include evaluating on-page components, specialized Website optimization factors, and backlink profiles. By leading thorough reviews, organizations can reveal open doors for development and forestall issues that could adversely influence web search tool rankings.

As the advanced scene develops, versatile Website design enhancement investigations have acquired unmistakable quality. With the rising utilization of cell phones, guaranteeing a dynamic site is essential. Versatile Search engine optimization examinations evaluate factors like portable page speed, responsive plan, and versatile ease of use, giving bits of knowledge into improving the developing portable crowd.

Online entertainment combination is one more component of Web optimization estimation. While social signs may not straightforwardly influence search rankings, a solid social presence can add to mark perceivability and commitment. Observing web-based entertainment measurements, like likes, offers, and remarks, assists organizations with figuring out the effect of their virtual entertainment endeavors on by and large internet based perceivability.

All in all, Website design enhancement examination and estimation are basic for organizations endeavoring to prevail in the serious web-based scene. From watchword investigation to transformation following, an all encompassing way to deal with Web optimization examination gives the essential bits of knowledge to refine techniques, further develop site execution, and at last accomplish business objectives. A sustainable and efficient SEO strategy in the dynamic digital environment is ensured by regular monitoring, adaptation, and optimization based on analytics data.

Key Metrics to Track and Tools for SEO Analysis

Site improvement (Search engine optimization) is urgent for online achievement, and keeping steady over key measurements is fundamental for advancing your site's exhibition. You can evaluate the success of your SEO efforts and make well-informed decisions to boost your website's visibility by keeping an eye on these metrics. Furthermore, using the right devices can smooth out the investigation cycle, giving important experiences into your site's Website optimization wellbeing.

Key Measurements to Track:

Natural Traffic:

Measure the quantity of guests coming to your site through natural pursuit. Instruments like Google Investigation can assist with following this measurement, providing you with an outline of how well your Website optimization systems are driving traffic.

Watchword Rankings:

Watch out for your site's positioning for designated catchphrases. Instruments, for example, SEMrush or Ahrefs give itemized experiences into watchword positions, permitting you to streamline your substance for better rankings.

Active clicking factor (CTR):

Examine the level of clients who click on your site from web search tool results. A higher CTR shows that your title labels and meta depictions are convincing. Google Search Control center is an important instrument for following CTR.

Rate of Bounce:

Assess the level of guests who explore away from your site subsequent to survey just a single page. A high skip rate might flag issues with your substance or client experience.

Page Burden Speed:

Client experience is a basic positioning variable. Google's PageSpeed Experiences can help you evaluate and upgrade your site's stacking speed for both work area and cell phones.

Backlink Profile:

Screen the quality and amount of backlinks highlighting your site. Instruments like Moz and Superb can give experiences into your backlink profile, assisting you with recognizing potential open doors for external link establishment.

Change Rate:

Track the level of guests who complete wanted activities, like making a buy or finishing up a structure. If you want to know how your SEO efforts are affecting your company's overall objectives, this metric is essential.

Assessing Mobile-Friendliness:

With the rising utilization of cell phones, guarantee your site is versatile. Google's Dynamic Test can help you recognize and fix issues influencing versatile clients.

Domain Authority as well as Page Authority:

Moz's measurements, Page Authority and Space Authority, give a complete perspective on your site's general power and impact. Plan to expand these scores through quality substance and respectable backlinks.

Client Commitment Measurements:
Break down measurements like time nearby, pages per meeting, and social offers to comprehend how clients cooperate with your substance. Commitment is a positive sign for web crawlers.

SEO Analysis Tools:
Google Examination:
A flexible device that gives exhaustive experiences into site traffic, client conduct, and change measurements. It's fundamental for following natural traffic and client commitment.

Google Search Control center:
provides useful information about your website's performance in Google's search results. Screen search investigation, submit sitemaps, and recognize creep blunders to improve your site's perceivability.

SEMrush:
A strong across the board Search engine optimization tool compartment that covers catchphrase research, contender investigation, backlink following, and then some. SEMrush assists you with fine tuning your Web optimization methodology in light of complete information.

Ahrefs:
Known for its vigorous backlink investigation capacities, Ahrefs likewise gives watchword research, rank following, and site review devices. It's a

go-to asset for understanding your site's connection profile.

Moz:

Moz offers apparatuses like Moz Star and Moz Neighborhood, giving experiences into watchword rankings, backlinks, and nearby Search engine optimization. The Page Authority and Space Authority measurements are especially valuable for checking site authority.

Yoast Website optimization:

A famous WordPress module that guides in on-page Website design enhancement streamlining. It assists clients with streamlining content, meta labels, and gives intelligibility investigation to improve in general Search engine optimization execution.

PageSpeed Bits of knowledge:

Google's instrument to evaluate your site's page speed. It gives ideas to further develop load times, adding to better client experience and web index rankings.

BuzzSumo:

This is useful for finding content and figuring out what kind of content does well in your industry. Distinguish moving subjects and make content that resounds with your crowd.

Shouting Frog Website optimization Bug:

a website crawling tool that analyzes on-page elements in depth. It uncovers issues like broken joins, copy content, and missing meta labels.

Google Patterns:

Investigate moving themes and search inquiries after some time. This instrument is helpful for recognizing themes that are right now famous and pertinent to your crowd. You can modify your SEO strategy to meet the changing requirements of search engines and user expectations by consistently monitoring these important metrics and utilizing the appropriate tools. To maintain a strong online presence and achieve long-term SEO success, regular analysis and optimization are essential.

Monitoring and Adjusting Strategies

Checking and changing systems are fundamental parts of compelling navigation and objective accomplishment in different parts of life, from business and money to self-improvement. These cycles include routinely evaluating the advancement of an arrangement or drive, distinguishing expected difficulties, and making fundamental acclimations to guarantee progress with progress.

In the business domain, checking techniques frequently spin around key execution markers (KPIs) and measurements that give knowledge into the organization's exhibition. These measurements can incorporate monetary markers like income and productivity, functional measurements like creation effectiveness, and client related measurements like fulfillment and standards for dependability. Consistently following and investigating these markers empower organizations to remain informed about their exhibition and go with informed choices.

A manufacturing company, for instance, might keep an eye on how efficient its production is to make sure it meets quality standards and stays cost-effective. Assuming productivity begins to decline, the organization can examine the underlying driver, whether it's apparatus issues, labor force difficulties, or store network interruptions. The business can keep its edge in the market and avoid potential financial losses by quickly identifying and resolving these issues.

Investment strategies must be monitored and adjusted in the financial industry in order to maximize returns and manage risks. Financial backers regularly survey the presentation of their portfolios, investigating market patterns, monetary pointers, and company-explicit information. At the point when economic situations change or new data arises, financial backers might have to change their portfolios to line up with their monetary objectives and hazard resilience.

Additionally, people chasing after self-improvement objectives utilize checking and changing procedures to keep tabs on their development and roll out essential improvements. Whether it's a wellness plan, instructive pursuits, or profession objectives, routinely assessing one's headway takes into consideration variations to more readily suit developing conditions. For example, on the off chance that somebody is pursuing a wellness objective and notification of a level in their advancement, they could change their exercise routine daily schedule or sustenance intended to get through the stagnation.

In project management, it is essential to monitor and adjust strategies to keep projects on track and achieve their goals. Project directors utilize different devices and procedures to screen project progress, for example, Gantt graphs, achievement following, and ordinary notices. In the event that unforeseen difficulties emerge or on the other hand on the off chance that underlying suspicions demonstrate mistaken, project supervisors can change timetables, asset allotments, or undertaking degrees to keep the venture on course.

Flexibility is a vital part of successful observing and changing procedures. Successful endeavors are frequently distinguished from unsuccessful ones by the capacity to respond to shifting circumstances in a timely and informed manner. This flexibility requires checking for indications of deviation as well as the readiness to make very much educated changes.

One outstanding illustration of the significance of checking and changing systems is in the tech business, where the speed of development is fast, and market elements can move quickly. Organizations that consistently screen client input, mechanical progressions, and cutthroat scenes can change their item improvement and advertising methodologies as needs be. Inability to adjust in such a unique climate can prompt out of date quality or being overwhelmed by additional coordinated contenders.

Notwithstanding, it's vital to figure out some kind of harmony between watchful checking and automatic responses.

Overcompensating to each minor vacillation can prompt superfluous disturbances, while forgetting to change even with huge difficulties can bring about botched open doors or disappointment. Hence, a smart and key way to deal with checking and changing is fundamental.

All in all, checking and changing procedures are necessary to progress in different spaces, from business and money to self-improvement and venture the executives. Routinely evaluating execution, recognizing difficulties, and causing informed acclimations to guarantee that plans stay important and compelling notwithstanding evolving conditions. Whether in the corporate meeting room, the securities exchange, or special goals, the capacity to adjust and refine systems is a sign of effective undertakings.

Chapter 7 Emerging Trends in SEO

Emerging Trends in SEO
Search Engine Optimization (SEO) is an ever-evolving field, adapting to changes in search engine algorithms and user behaviors. In 2024, several emerging trends are shaping the landscape of SEO.

1. Your Situating's Component: the Client Experience (UX)

Search engines increasingly prioritize user experience. Factors like page load speed, mobile-friendliness, and overall website usability are critical. Sites that offer a seamless, enjoyable experience tend to rank higher.

2. Core Web Vitals and Page Experience:

Google's Core Web Vitals, focusing on loading performance, interactivity, and visual stability, have become crucial metrics. Websites that meet these criteria are more likely to rank higher, emphasizing the importance of optimizing for a smooth user experience.

3. Voice Search Optimization:

With the rise of voice-activated devices and virtual assistants, optimizing content for voice search is essential. Natural language processing and understanding user intent become pivotal for SEO success.

4. BERT Algorithm and Natural Language Processing:

Google's BERT (Bidirectional Encoder Representations from Transformers) algorithm aims to understand context and nuances in search queries better. Content creators need to focus on providing relevant, high-quality content that answers user queries effectively.

5. Video SEO and Visual Search:

Video content keeps on acquiring conspicuousness in query items. Optimizing videos for search engines, using relevant keywords, and providing detailed descriptions enhance visibility. Additionally, visual search, powered by AI, enables users to search using images, prompting the need for image optimization.

6. Structured Data Markup:

Search engines rely on structured data to understand content better. Implementing schema markup helps search engines comprehend the context of your content, potentially leading to enhanced rich snippets in search results.

7. Mobile-First Indexing:

As portable use keeps on rising, web search tools focus on versatile first ordering. Websites must be designed with mobile users in mind, ensuring a responsive design and consistent content across devices.

8. AI and Machine Learning in SEO:

SEO tactics are increasingly being influenced by AI and machine learning. Automation tools help analyze vast amounts of data, refine targeting, and personalize user experiences. Understanding and incorporating AI-driven insights are becoming essential for SEO professionals.

9. E-A-T (Expertise, Authoritativeness, Trustworthiness):

Google emphasizes the importance of E-A-T in evaluating content quality. Websites need to establish themselves as credible sources by showcasing expertise, building authority, and maintaining trustworthiness in their respective industries.

10. Local SEO and Google My Business Optimization:

(sql code)

Local search optimization remains crucial, especially for businesses targeting a specific geographic area. Optimizing Google My Business profiles, obtaining positive reviews, and providing accurate business information are key aspects of local SEO.

11. Content Clusters and Topic Authority:

(css code)

Instead of focusing on individual keywords, the trend is shifting towards creating content clusters around broader topics. Establishing topic authority through in-depth, comprehensive content can boost overall search visibility.

12. Zero-Click Searches and Featured Snippets:

(sq code)

Zero-click searches, where users obtain information directly from search results without clicking on a website, are on the rise. Optimizing for featured snippets can help websites secure prime positions in search results.

Staying ahead in the dynamic landscape of SEO requires adapting to emerging trends. Prioritizing user experience, embracing new technologies, and creating valuable, authoritative content are key strategies for success in 2024 and beyond.

Voice Search Optimization

As the number of devices with voice capabilities continues to rise, Voice Search Optimization (VSO) is an essential component of contemporary digital marketing strategies. With the multiplication of remote helpers like Siri, Google Collaborator, and Alexa, buyers are progressively depending on voice searches to interface with innovation. In this scene, organizations should adjust their web-based presence to guarantee perceivability and pertinence in voice query items.

One key distinction among text and voice look through lies in the client's question structure. While text looks frequently composed of succinct catchphrases, voice inquiries will generally be more conversational and regular. Subsequently, upgrading for voice search requires a change in Website design enhancement procedures. Long-tail catchphrases and expressions that copy communicated in language become vital in catching the subtleties of voice questions.

Understanding client plans is fundamental in VSO. Voice looks are in many cases driven by a quick requirement for data, administrations, or items. Consequently, satisfaction ought to be organized to address explicit client questions actually. Making FAQs that line up with potential voice search questions improves the possibilities showing up in applicable outcomes.

Voice Search Optimization has the potential to significantly benefit local businesses in particular. Many voice looks are area explicit, for example, "cafés close to me" or "closest service station." Improving neighborhood Website design enhancement components, for example, Google My Professional resources and area based watchwords, assists organizations with exploiting voice search traffic and draw in adjacent clients.

Organized information markup, as schema.org, is a fundamental part of VSO. By furnishing web search tools with clear data about your substance, items, or administrations, you improve the probability of being highlighted in voice indexed lists. This organized information can incorporate subtleties like business hours, contact data, and item determinations, making it more straightforward for remote helpers to concentrate and present important data.

Site speed and versatile enhancement are basic variables in voice search positioning. Voice looks frequently happen on cell phones, and clients anticipate fast and consistent outcomes. Slow-stacking sites might prompt client disappointment and diminishing the probability of being suggested in future voice look. Guaranteeing your site is versatile and advanced for speed upgrades the general client experience and decidedly influences VSO.

Regular language handling (NLP) assumes an essential part in voice search calculations. Remote helpers are turning out to be progressively modern in understanding the subtleties of human language, making it basic for organizations to create content that lines up with these headways. Creating content that addresses explicit inquiries succinctly and conversationally improves its similarity with voice search calculations.

Voice search examinations give significant experiences into client conduct. By examining the examples and patterns in voice look through connected with your industry or specialty, organizations can refine their VSO techniques. Observing the exhibition of explicit catchphrases, following client plans, and adjusting content in view of arising patterns add to a more successful voice inquiry improvement approach.

Online entertainment presence is likewise interwoven with VSO. On platforms like Facebook, Twitter, and Instagram, where people frequently use voice commands, it is essential for businesses to maintain an engaging social media presence. A brand's overall online authority can be influenced by social signals like likes, shares, and comments, which can also have an effect on voice search rankings.

Businesses should take into account voice commerce, or v-commerce, in their VSO efforts. As remote helpers become more incorporated into internet business stages, streamlining item postings for voice look becomes vital. This includes giving nitty gritty item data, clear invitations to take action, and a consistent buying process through voice orders.

All in all, Voice Inquiry Improvement is a dynamic and developing field that requests an essential methodology from organizations. Adjusting to the conversational idea of voice inquiries, streamlining for nearby ventures, utilizing organized information markup, and keeping up to date with innovative progressions are indispensable parts of an effective VSO technique. As voice-empowered gadgets keep on molding the advanced scene, organizations that focus on and put resources into Voice

Inquiry Improvement will hang out in an undeniably serious web-based climate.

Featured Snippets and Position Zero

In the always advancing scene of site improvement (Web optimization), it is vital to acquire perceivability. One key region that has accumulated critical consideration as of late is the sought after "Position Zero," which is much of the time involved by Highlighted Bits. Understanding these components is vital for advertisers and site proprietors endeavoring to improve their internet based presence.

An Overview of the Featured Snippets:

Highlighted Scraps are compact, explicit replies that Google shows at the highest point of its query items, over the ordinary natural postings. They mean to furnish clients with fast and important data without expecting them to navigate to a particular site. These pieces commonly show up because of search inquiries expressed as questions, for example, "How to," "What is," or "Why."

Kinds of Highlighted Bits:

Passage Scraps: These scraps present data in a concise passage design, giving a speedy solution to the client's question.

List Pieces: Data introduced in a rundown design is one more typical kind of Highlighted Bit. Recipes, step-by-step guides, and other content that can be arranged in a list all work well in this format.

Table Scraps: At the point when data is best addressed in a plain organization, Google might show a table piece. This is frequently seen for information correlations, item particulars, and comparable substance.

How Google Chooses Highlighted Pieces:
Google's calculations figure out which content should be included. The relevance and quality of the content, the page's structure, and the user experience as a whole all play a role in this decision. It is essential to keep in mind that Google always attributes the information it uses in Featured Snippets to previously published web pages.

Upgrading for Highlighted Scraps:
Give Unmistakable responses: Create satisfied with clear, compact solutions to normal client inquiries. Expecting and resolving potential inquiries can build the possibilities of procuring a Highlighted Scrap.

Utilize Organized Markup: Carrying out organized information markup on your site can assist with looking through motors to better grasp the substance. The way Featured Snippets are shown can be affected by this markup.

Make Excellent Substance: Google focuses on legitimate and efficient substances. Guarantee that your pages are elegantly composed, instructive, and applicable to client questions.

Understanding Position Zero:
Position No alludes to the arrangement of Highlighted Scraps at the highest point of the list items, making them the main thing clients see. Accomplishing Position Zero is profoundly attractive as it can fundamentally expand

perceivability and drive more natural traffic to a site.

Advantages of Position Zero:

Increased Attraction: Content shown in Place Zero is unmistakably highlighted, making it bound to grab the client's eye and produce clicks.

Authority and Trust: Procuring an Included Scrap positions a site as a definitive source on a specific point, imparting trust among clients.

Voice Inquiry Enhancement: With the ascent of voice search, Position Zero turns out to be much more basic. Voice associates frequently pull answers straightforwardly from Included Pieces.

Difficulties of Highlighted Scraps:

Diminished Navigate Rates: While Included Bits improve perceivability, they can prompt lower navigate rates, as clients might find the data they need without visiting the source site.

Dynamic Character: Featured Snippet rankings fluctuate as a result of Google's algorithmic improvements. Keeping up to date with these progressions is fundamental for keeping up with Position Zero.

Procedures for Winning Position Zero:

Determine Target Questions: Find queries that are relevant to your content and are likely to result in Featured Snippets by conducting research.

Produce extensive content: Foster substance that completely answers the objective inquiries. This improves the probability of Google choosing your substance for Position Zero.

Optimize for Keywords with Long Tails: Long-tail catchphrases frequently lead to additional particular inquiries, making it simpler to enhance content for Highlighted Bits.

Highlighted Scraps and Position Zero have reshaped the Web optimization scene, underlining the significance of giving fast, pertinent responses to client inquiries. While the difficulties are obvious, the advantages of expanded perceivability and authority put forth the attempt beneficial. Staying up to date on the most effective methods for optimizing content for Featured Snippets is essential for anyone who wants to succeed in today's highly competitive online environment.

AI and Machine Learning in SEO

The field of Search Engine Optimization (SEO) has been transformed by AI and machine learning, which have provided marketers and businesses with potent tools for increasing their online visibility. These innovations influence information investigation, design acknowledgment, and mechanization to advance different parts of Search engine optimization, eventually further developing site rankings and client experience.

Utilizing machine learning algorithms to gain a deeper comprehension of search engine algorithms is one significant SEO application of AI. With AI, algorithms can analyze vast amounts of data to identify patterns and correlations that influence search engine rankings. Traditional SEO strategies typically required manual keyword optimization and link building. This empowers advertisers to settle on additional educated conclusions about happy creation, watchword focusing on, and in general enhancement procedures.

Content creation is a significant part of Website optimization, and man-made intelligence has demonstrated to be an important partner in this space. Normal Language Handling (NLP) calculations empower machines to grasp and produce human-like text, working with the production of great and applicable substances. Simulated intelligence controlled content age devices can deliver articles, blog entries, and item portrayals, saving time and assets for organizations while keeping an emphasis on Web optimization cordial substance.

Understanding user preferences and behavior also relies on machine learning algorithms. By examining information connected with client communications with sites, web crawlers can adjust and customize query items in light of individual inclinations. This customized approach upgrades client experience and improves the probability of clients drawing in with the substance, which thus decidedly influences Web optimization rankings.

Chatbots and virtual assistants powered by AI are now standard features of online customer interactions. These apparatuses improve client commitment by giving moment reactions to questions, directing clients through sites, and proposing customized proposals. Search engines take into account factors like longer dwell times and lower bounce rates when determining the quality and relevance of a website when users are more engaged.

The development of man-made intelligence has achieved picture and video acknowledgment abilities, affecting Website design enhancement methodologies in media content improvement. Computer based intelligence calculations can examine and grasp the substance inside pictures and recordings, permitting web crawlers to list and rank media content precisely. This is especially critical for organizations working in outwardly determined businesses, as it empowers them to upgrade their web-based presence through mixed media content.

Voice search has acquired conspicuousness with the multiplication of menial helpers like Siri and Alexa. Simulated intelligence is instrumental in understanding and answering voice questions, affecting how sites are improved for search. Advertisers presently need to consider conversational catchphrases and long-tail expressions that line up with how clients talk as opposed to type. Businesses must adjust their SEO strategies to accommodate this changing search behavior as voice search continues to grow.

Computer based intelligence calculations additionally add to better site execution through prescient investigation. By examining verifiable information and client designs, artificial intelligence can foresee future patterns and assist advertisers with expecting changes in web crawler calculations or client conduct. This proactive methodology empowers organizations to remain in front of the opposition and adjust their Website design enhancement techniques in a similar manner.

AI helps automate routine SEO tasks, in addition to predictive analytics. This incorporates errands, for example, watchword research, rank following, and execution investigation. Not only does automation conserve time, but it also lowers the likelihood of human error. Website design enhancement experts can zero in on additional essential parts of advancement while computer based intelligence handles the dull assignments productively.

Nonetheless, it's fundamental to recognize the difficulties related with the combination of simulated intelligence and AI in Website design enhancement. The fast development of calculations represents a consistent test for advertisers to remain refreshed and adjust their techniques as needs be. In addition, moral contemplations with respect to client protection and information security should be tended to as man-made intelligence depends vigorously on information examination.

The landscape of digital marketing has been transformed by the incorporation of AI and machine learning into SEO. From content creation and personalization to picture acknowledgment and prescient investigation, simulated intelligence has turned into a main thrust behind effective Search engine optimization systems. Organizations that hug and influence these innovations stand to acquire an upper hand in the consistently developing web-based climate. Marketers will need to remain adaptable and creative in their approach as AI continues to advance, and its influence on SEO will undoubtedly grow.

Chapter 8
Case Studies
Successful
SEO
Campaigns

Disclosing the Privileged insights of Fruitful Website optimization Missions

In the steadily developing scene of online perceivability, becoming amazing at Website improvement (Web optimization) is essential for organizations meaning to flourish in the advanced domain. Effective Website design enhancement crusades are set apart by essential preparation, versatile procedures, and a profound comprehension of web crawler calculations. We should dig into a couple of contextual investigations that enlighten the pathways to Web optimization win.

1. Moz's Whiteboard Friday:

Moz, an unmistakable player in the Web optimization industry, carried out a profoundly effective mission known as "Whiteboard Friday." This drive included making sagacious video content, highlighting industry specialists handling assorted Website optimization subjects. By reliably conveying significant data, Moz upgraded its web-based authority as well as encouraged local area commitment. The mission's prosperity lay in its obligation to teaching the crowd, laying out Moz as a go-to asset for Website design enhancement information.

2. Airbnb's Restriction Methodology:

Airbnb's worldwide achievement is incompletely credited to its successful limitation technique. Perceiving the meaning of territorial pursuit patterns, Airbnb advanced its site for neighborhood dialects and altered content in view of clients' topographical areas. Their visibility in a variety of markets was significantly enhanced by this granular SEO strategy, demonstrating the significance of tailoring SEO efforts to various audiences.

3. Dollar Shave Club's Substance Brightness:

Not only did Dollar Shave Club's innovative product cause a disruption in the grooming industry, but it also implemented a content-focused SEO strategy. By making amusing and shareable substance, for example, the viral "Our Edges Are F***ing Extraordinary" video, the organization earned boundless consideration and significant backlinks.

This case highlights the power of convincing substance in driving natural rush hour gridlock and building major areas of strength for a presence.

4. HubSpot's Point of support Page Methodology:

HubSpot's fruitful Website optimization crusade included the execution of support point pages - far reaching, theme bunch pages that cover a wide subject and connection to more top to bottom substance. This key interlinking improved client experience as well as lined up with web crawler calculations inclining toward content profundity and importance.

HubSpot's methodology exhibited the force of a very much organized content pecking order in supporting Search engine optimization execution.

5. The Google Penguin Recuperation by iPage:

Numerous websites were hit hard with ranking penalties as a result of Google's Penguin algorithm update. iPage, a web facilitating supplier, dealt with this challenge directly by leading an intensive review of its backlink profile and taking out malicious connections.

Through industrious endeavors to agree with Google's rules, iPage effectively recuperated its rankings. For long-term SEO success, this case demonstrates the significance of staying vigilant and adapting strategies to algorithmic changes.

All in all, the domain of fruitful Web optimization crusades is huge and multi-layered. Whether through instructive substance, restricted techniques, connecting with content, or versatile ways to deal with algorithmic movements, these contextual investigations enlighten the assorted pathways to Web optimization win.

Organizations trying to explore the computerized scene should perceive the unique idea of Web optimization and embrace systems that line up with both client aim and web index calculations.

Lessons Learned from SEO Failures

Website design enhancement disappointments can be a significant wellspring of bits of knowledge, directing organizations toward additional compelling systems. In the unique scene of site design improvement, botches are unavoidable, yet the examples gained from these difficulties can be groundbreaking. Here are key important points from normal Web optimization disappointments.

Overlooking Client Experience (UX):
One predominant mix-up is ignoring the significance of client experience. Google progressively esteems sites that offer a consistent, easy to understand insight. Slow-stacking pages, befuddling routes, or nosy advertisements can obstruct client fulfillment and affect search rankings. Focusing on UX helps Search engine optimization as well as improves generally consumer loyalty.

Watchword Stuffing:
Keyword stuffing was a common way to manipulate search rankings in the early days of SEO. In any case, search calculations have developed, and catchphrase stuffing is presently punished. The takeaway from this is to concentrate on writing content that is of high quality, is relevant, and naturally

incorporates keywords. Take a stab at an offset that reverberates with both web indexes and human perusers.

Mobile optimization is ignored:

With the rising utilization of cell phones, portable streamlining is presently not discretionary. Disregarding this viewpoint can bring about lower search rankings, as Google focuses on dynamic sites. Embracing responsive plans and guaranteeing a consistent encounter across gadgets is vital for Website design enhancement achievement.

Sitting above Nearby Website optimization:

Numerous organizations misjudge the force of neighborhood search. Dismissing neighborhood Search engine optimization techniques, for example, advancing Google My Professional resources, can prompt botched open doors. Perceiving the meaning of nearby quests and fitting substance likewise is fundamental for organizations with an actual presence.

Disregarding Specialized Website optimization:

Specialized Web optimization issues, like broken joins, copy content, or unfortunate site structure, can fundamentally affect search rankings. Routinely evaluating and resolving specialized issues is essential for keeping a sound site and improving for web crawlers.

Not Focusing on Quality Backlinks:

While backlinks are vital for Website design enhancement, the accentuation ought to be on higher standards no matter what. Your website's reputation and rankings may suffer if you acquire spammy or low-quality backlinks. Center around building a different and normal connection profile through trustworthy sources to upgrade your site's position.

Inability to Adjust to Calculation Changes:

Web index calculations are continually developing. Rankings can drop suddenly if you don't keep up with changes and adjust your strategies accordingly. Staying versatile and proactive in light of calculation changes is critical to long haul Website design enhancement achievement.

Insufficient Content Strategy:

Content is the foundation of Website optimization, and an absence of a lucid substance technique can be unfavorable. Delivering content without an unmistakable concentration, significance, or worth to the crowd may not yield the ideal outcomes. Foster a complete substance technique that lines up with client goals and industry patterns.

Not Observing Investigation:

Without normal observing of site investigation, evaluating the viability of Website optimization efforts is testing. Disregarding information can prompt botched open doors for development. Reliably dissect execution measurements, for example, traffic sources, bob rates, and transformation rates, to go with informed choices.

Depending Entirely on Natural Traffic:

While natural traffic is critical, depending entirely on it tends to be unsafe. Enhance your traffic sources by consolidating paid promoting, web-based entertainment, and different channels. This not just mitigates the effect of potential calculation changes yet additionally expands your generally online presence.

Misjudging the Significance of On-Page Website design enhancement:

On-page Website design enhancement components, including title labels, meta depictions, and header labels, assume a significant part in search rankings. Dismissing these parts can obstruct a site's perceivability. Focus on-page Website design enhancement best practices to advance each piece of content for web crawlers.

Anxiety with Results:

Website design enhancement is a drawn out system, and results may not be immediate. Eagerness and a craving for fast wins can prompt hurried choices and less than ideal strategies. Set sensible assumptions, put resources into feasible techniques, and comprehend that Website design enhancement achievement takes time.

All in all, Website design enhancement disappointments are unavoidable, however the illustrations separated from these mishaps can shape a stronger and successful procedure. By focusing on client experience, remaining informed about industry changes, and reliably refining your methodology, organizations can explore the intricacies of Website design enhancement with better progress.

CONCLUSION

Strategies and Continuous Adaptation in SEO

All in all, Website streamlining (Search engine optimization) remains as a basic foundation in the computerized scene, filling in as a compass for organizations and people looking for improved web-based perceivability. The procedures utilized in Web optimization are complex, enveloping a scope of strategies intended to further develop natural hunt rankings. As the web keeps on advancing, Web optimization stays a crucial device for those endeavoring to remain ahead in the exceptionally cutthroat computerized domain.

The improvement of organic search rankings is one of the main goals of SEO, which is done by using a variety of strategies. Watchword streamlining, for example, assumes an urgent part in guaranteeing that a site lines up with the pursuit questions clients ordinarily input. By carefully choosing and consolidating significant catchphrases all through the site's substance, meta labels, and different components, organizations can support their possibilities positioning higher in web crawler results.

Content quality arises as one more foundation in Web optimization achievement. Web crawlers, driven by client fulfillment, focus on sites that offer significant, important, and connecting content. Thus, making great substance that takes care of the requirements of the main interest group further develops natural inquiry rankings as well as adds to laying out the validity and authority of a site inside its specialty.

Backlinks, or inbound connections from other trustworthy sites, use significant impact over a site's web index rankings. Backlinks are seen by search engines as a sign of confidence, indicating that the linked content is valuable and reliable. A powerful backlink system includes gaining joins from definitive sources, encouraging an organization of associations that can fundamentally hoist a site's natural hunt standing.

Specialized Web optimization components are similarly urgent in the journey for further developed search rankings. Upgrading site speed, guaranteeing versatile responsiveness, and improving webpage engineering add to a positive client experience, factors that web search tools consider while positioning sites. Specialized Web optimization fills in as the spine, guaranteeing that a site meets as well as surpasses the norms set via web crawler calculations.

For businesses that have a physical location, local SEO strategies are absolutely necessary. A Google My Business profile, positive reviews, and accurate business information across various online platforms are all part of optimizing for local searches. Nearby

Website optimization upgrades perceivability in area explicit pursuits, making it a basic device for physical foundations planning to draw in neighborhood customers.

The scene of Website design enhancement is dynamic, with web crawlers ceaselessly refining their calculations. Keeping up to date with these progressions is principal for keeping up with and further developing natural inquiry rankings. Constantly refreshing and reviving substance, adjusting to new algorithmic contemplations, and embracing arising patterns, for example, voice inquiry improvement are essential for supporting an upper hand in the steadily developing computerized circle.

As organizations and people explore the intricacies of Website design enhancement, the significance of investigation couldn't possibly be more significant. SEO strategies can be evaluated based on the performance of key performance indicators (KPIs). Measurements like natural traffic, skip rates, and change rates give important bits of knowledge into the effect of Website design enhancement endeavors, empowering ideal acclimations to advance execution constantly.

While natural pursuit rankings are a critical part of Website optimization, perceivability reaches out past customary web search tools. Web-based entertainment stages are fundamental to a general computerized presence, and their effect on search rankings ought to be acknowledged with a sober mind. Through increased online visibility and brand mentions, engaging in social media marketing can not only increase brand awareness but also indirectly contribute to SEO success.

Taking on moral Website optimization rehearses is fundamental for supported achievement. In order to combat manipulative practices and ensure an online environment that is just and centered on users, search engines constantly improve their algorithms. Taking part in dark cap Web optimization strategies, for example, catchphrase stuffing or shrouding, may yield transient gains yet conveys the gamble of extreme punishments, including being deindexed from web crawler results.

All in all, the domain of Search engine optimization is a dynamic and multi-layered scene where procedures persistently develop in light of changing calculations and client ways of behaving. From fastidious catchphrase streamlining to the development of top notch content and the essential securing of backlinks, the excursion to further developed natural pursuit rankings requests a comprehensive methodology. The impact of SEO efforts is further amplified when technical aspects are taken into account, local considerations are taken into account, and social media is incorporated into the overall strategy.

The fundamental objective remains the same regardless of whether individuals or businesses become involved in the intricacies of SEO: to improve online perceivability. If you want to succeed in the vast and ever-expanding world of the internet, mastering the art and science of search engine optimization (SEO) is not just a choice; rather, it is a strategic necessity.

DEAR READER

Your thoughts matter to us! If the book brought a smile or moment of respite, please Consider Sharing your experience through a review.

Your feedback is invaluable in making our book even more enjoyable for following.We hope this message finds you well and enjoying your literary adventures! We value the opinions of our readers, and we would love to hear your thoughts on **[SEARCH ENGINE OPTIMIZATION (SEO)]**.

Thank you for being a part of our literary journey, and we look forward to reading your review!

WARM REGARDS

www.ingramcontent.com/pod-product-compliance
Lightning Source LLC
LaVergne TN
LVHW051701050326
832903LV00032B/3932